# MILLENNIAL WEALTH

# MILLENNIAL WEALTH

## 42 FINANCIAL TIPS FOR A SECURE FUTURE

JASMINE WILLIAMS

# TABLE OF CONTENTS

# UNDERSTANDING MILLENNIAL MONEY MINDSETS: OVERCOMING STEREOTYPES

## The Key Ideas

The millennial generation, born between 1981 and 1996, often faces stereotypes about their financial habits. These include misconceptions such as being poor savers, the 'avocado toast' generation, and having a sense of entitlement. However, the truth behind their money mindset is more complex, influenced by factors such as economic recessions, student loan debt, and changes in job markets.

Millennials are:

• **Tech-Savvy**: They prioritize online banking, investing apps, and the use of technology for financial management.

• **Value Experiences**: They prefer spending on experiences over material possessions, reflecting a shift in what constitutes 'value'.

• **Ethically-Conscious**: Investments tend to align with personal values; they support businesses that are socially and environmentally responsible.

- **Seek Financial Education**: They actively seek information and education about personal finance, often through online platforms.

## Practical Implementation

To align with millennial money mindsets:

1. **Budget with Flexibility**: Make use of budgeting apps to track and adjust spending. Allow for experience-related expenses while cutting back on unnecessary items.

2. **Tech-Enhanced Savings**: Automate savings through apps that round up purchases or transfer small amounts to savings regularly.

3. **Invest with Purpose**: Research and invest in funds or companies that match personal values, e.g., sustainable energy, fair trade.

4. **Seek Education and Mentorship**: Take online courses, read recent publications, and seek mentorship for personal finance education.

5. **Start Small with Investing**: Use micro-investing platforms to begin investing with small amounts of money, which can significantly grow over time.

## Consistency and Evaluation

To maintain a healthy financial lifestyle and continue growing wealth, millennials should:

- **Review Finances Regularly**: Set monthly or quarterly intervals to assess financial health and adjust strategies accordingly.

- **Measure Progress Against Goals**: Establish clear, achievable financial goals and use benchmarks to measure progress.

- **Seek Feedback**: Have dialogues with financial coaches or peers to gain insights and perspectives, which may lead to improved strategies.

**Evaluate Ethical Investments**: Continuously research and reassess the impact of investments to ensure they stay aligned with evolving personal values.

By understanding and incorporating these principles, millennials can overcome stereotypes and establish robust, sustainable financial practices for the future.

# FINANCIAL ADULTING: SETTING UP YOUR BUDGET FOR SUCCESS

## The Key Ideas

Budgeting isn't merely a task; it's a pivotal skill for financial self-reliance. Proper budgeting enables you to prioritize your spending, track where every dollar goes, and set clear goals saving for future needs. Here are the foundational principles:

- **Income vs. Expenses**: Understand every source of your income. List your expenses, categorizing them into necessities and luxuries.

- **The 50/30/20 Rule**: Allocate 50% of your income to needs, 30% to wants, and save or invest the remaining 20%.

- **S.M.A.R.T. Goals**: Specific, Measurable, Achievable, Relevant, Time-bound objectives anchor your financial actions.

- **Flexibility**: A good budget adapts to unforeseen changes. Maintain a buffer within your plan.

- **Tools and Resources**: Utilize apps and online services to streamline the budgeting process.

- **The Power of Habit**: Regular budgeting becomes less daunting when it's part of your routine.

# Practical Implementation

To convert these ideas into action, you must follow a structured approach:

1. **Assess Your Financial Health**: Begin by compiling a detailed list of monthly income and expenses. Separate wants from needs.

2. **Create Your Budget Blueprint**: Using the 50/30/20 rule as a guideline, allocate your funds accordingly within your personal income brackets.

3. **Automate Savings**: Set up automatic transfers to your savings account on payday.

4. **Track Your Spending**: Regularly monitor your expenditure by keeping receipts or using an app.

5. **Review and Adjust**: At the end of each month, review your budget and make necessary adjustments.

# Consistency and Evaluation

Budgeting is not a set-and-forget process. It requires periodic reviews and modifications:

- **Monthly Check-ins**: Dedicate time each month to review your spending patterns and adjust the budget as needed.

- **Expense Categorization**: Always look for ways to categorize expenses more accurately for better tracking and analysis.

- **Annual Review**: At least once a year, perform a detailed evaluation of your financial goals and the efficacy of your budget.

Remember, the aim is to create a budget that works for you, not the other way around. Your financial journey is uniquely yours; craft your budget to help you navigate it successfully.

# THE ART OF BALANCING INCOME AND EXPENSES

## The Key Ideas

**Financial stability hinges on equilibrium**: your financial health is defined by the balance between money flowing in and going out. Mastering this equilibrium is less about massive earning or extreme frugality, and more about smart management.

- **Develop a clear picture of your income**: understand the entirety of your earnings, which includes your salary, freelance payments, investments, and any passive income sources.

- **Reality-check your expenses**: gather up-to-date information on your fixed costs (rent, utilities, subscriptions) and variable expenses (groceries, entertainment, miscellaneous purchases).

- **Set immediate and long-term goals**: prioritize what's urgent (debt repayment) and what's important (saving for a house) to guide your budgeting.

- **Utilize effective tools**: digital budgeting apps, online financial trackers, and traditional spreadsheets can help maintain oversight.

# Practical Implementation

**Track and Categorize**: Begin by meticulously recording every income and expense over a month to understand your financial habits.

1. List all income sources, noting their frequency and reliability.

2. Categorize expenses as 'needs' (essentials) or 'wants' (non-essentials).

3. Monitor casual spending that often goes unchecked (e.g., coffee on the go, ride-shares).

**Budget with Purpose**: Use the information gathered to formulate a budget that reflects your values and goals.

- Allocate income to savings before anything else—consider it a non-negotiable expense.

- Adjust your spending habits to align with your goals, perhaps using the 50/30/20 rule as a benchmark (50% on needs, 30% on wants, 20% on savings).

- Cut down on 'wants' progressively; avoid abrupt changes that are unsustainable.

**Reduce and Optimize Expenses**:

- Swap out high-cost services for more affordable alternatives without sacrificing quality (e.g., streaming services, phone plans).

- Use shopping lists to curb impulsive purchases; stick to them strictly.

- Implement energy-saving practices to lower utility bills.

**Grow Your Income**: Consider ways to enhance your earning potential.

- Take on freelance work, if feasible.

- Seek professional development to improve job prospects and raise your market value.

- Explore passive income opportunities, such as investing in dividend-paying stocks or real estate.

## Consistency and Evaluation

Maintaining balance is an ongoing process. Continual review of income and expenses, coupled with adjustments to your budget, keeps you aligned with your financial targets.

**Regular Check-ins**: Set a specific day each week or month for reviewing your budget and evaluate your progress.

- Assess if you're meeting your savings goals.

- Identify any new or rising expenses and adjust accordingly.

- Reflect on whether your financial habits are moving you closer to or further from your objectives.

**Annual Reviews**:

- Conduct a comprehensive annual review that accounts for changes in income, life stages, and goals.

- Update your financial plan to accommodate any major shifts such as a new job, marriage, or the birth of a child.

**Stay Informed**:

- Keep up with economic trends that could impact your investments or job security.

• Educate yourself on personal finance regularly to hone your skills in managing money efficiently.

**Flexibility Is Key**: Be prepared to pivot and make changes to your budget and spending as life happens.

• Adapt to unexpected expenses without derailing your financial goals.

• Make room for occasional indulgences; a balanced life includes enjoying the present while planning for the future.

Balancing income and expenses is not a one-time task but a lifelong approach. It transitions as you transition, through different life stages and financial milestones. The true art lies in creating a flexible system that adapts to your evolving needs, helping you secure a prosperous and stress-free future.

# EMERGENCY FUNDS: YOUR FINANCIAL SAFETY NET

## The Key Ideas

An emergency fund is an essential pillar in the foundation of financial security. It serves as a buffer against unforeseen expenses such as medical emergencies, car repairs, or sudden job loss. Building and maintaining this fund is a proactive step toward financial resilience.

**Why Emergency Funds Are Crucial:**

- Provides financial security during unexpected events.

- Reduces the need for high-interest debt in emergencies.

- Offers peace of mind, which is invaluable.

**Ideal Size of An Emergency Fund:**

- Aim for 3 to 6 months' worth of living expenses.

- Adjust based on individual circumstances like job stability.

**Where to Keep Your Emergency Fund:**

- Accessible, but not too easy to spend impulsively (e.g., a savings account).

- Consider high-yield savings accounts for better interest accumulation.

# Practical Implementation

Setting up an emergency fund isn't complicated, but it requires discipline. Start with these steps:

1. **Assess Your Monthly Living Expenses:**

   - Calculate necessities like housing, food, transportation, and utilities.

2. **Determine Your Target Fund Size:**

   - Base it on your assessed living expenses and personal comfort level.

3. **Establish a Separate Savings Account:**

   - Use an account solely dedicated to emergencies.

4. **Start Small:**

   - Even a small initial deposit can be the seed that grows into a full-fledged emergency fund.

5. **Automate Contributions:**

   - Schedule automatic transfers to your emergency fund after each paycheck.

6. **Cut Unnecessary Spending:**

   - Identify luxuries you can live without and channel those savings into your emergency fund.

7. **Use Windfalls Wisely:**

   - Allocate at least a portion of bonuses, tax refunds, or gifts to bolster your fund.

# Consistency and Evaluation

Building an emergency fund is a marathon, not a sprint. Consistently contribute and periodically assess your fund.

- **Review your fund size annually:**

    ○ Adjust for changes in income or living expenses.

- **Keep contributions steady:**

    ○ Continue automatic transfers, even when you reach your initial goal.

- **Increase contributions if possible:**

    ○ As your income grows, so should your fund—aim to strengthen that financial safety net.

- **Resist Temptation:**

    ○ Only use the fund for genuine emergencies to maintain its integrity.

An emergency fund is not glamorous, but it's one of the most responsible steps you can take in managing your personal finances. By adhering to these principles and establishing a solid financial safety net, you're securing not just your finances, but also your future.

# THE MYTH OF THE LATTE FACTOR: SMART SMALL SPENDINGS

## The Key Ideas

- **Latte Factor Revisited**: The belief that skipping small indulgences like daily lattes can lead to significant savings over time. This concept, popularized by financial authors, implies cutting out minor luxuries to boost savings.

- **Reality Check**: Elimination of small joys may not lead to substantial wealth accumulation, as it often overlooks the broader aspects of financial management.

- **Value of Happiness**: Minor expenditures on treats such as lattes can enhance daily happiness and productivity, which may, in turn, support better financial decisions.

- **Intelligent Small Spending**: Smart small spendings mean understanding the true value these purchases bring to your life and finding a balance that aligns with your personal and financial goals.

- **Budget Alignment**: Ensure small spendings align with your budget without jeopardizing your financial objectives.

- **Investment Vs. Instant Gratification**: Differentiate between spendings that are purely for instant gratification and those that have long-term benefits, like investing in networking opportunities or personal development.

## Practical Implementation

1. **Budget for Joy**: Allocate a specific budget for small pleasures within your overall financial plan.

2. **Mindful Spending**:

   - Keep track of these small expenses.

   - Ask whether they contribute to overall satisfaction or are impulsive buys.

3. **Quality Over Quantity**: Opt for fewer high-quality experiences over daily indulgences that may add up financially without adding much to quality of life.

4. **Annual Review**: Look at your small spendings over a year. See if they align with your happiness and financial goals.

5. **Embrace Technology**: Use budgeting apps or financial software to monitor small spendings without making it a tedious task.

## Consistency and Evaluation

- **Regular Check-Ins**: Assess your small spendings monthly. Adjust as necessary to stay on track with your goals.

- **Happy Savings**: Recognize when cutting small spendings diminishes your quality of life. If the impact on happiness is too great, reassess your approach.

- **Long-term Perspective**: Evaluate how these small purchases fit into your long-term wealth-building strategy, including investments and savings goals.

• **Sustainable Choices**: Make small spending decisions that you can sustain over time without feeling deprived or causing financial strain.

• **Seek Balance**: The goal is not to cut out all joy but to find a balance that allows for small pleasures while advancing towards financial security.

# CAREER MOVES: NEGOTIATING SALARY AND BENEFITS

## The Key Ideas

**Understand Your Worth:** Knowing your market value is crucial. Use resources like Glassdoor, PayScale, and LinkedIn Salary to research what others in your position with similar experience are earning. Ensure you're aware of your industry, location, and experience level.

**The Whole Package:** Salary is just one part of the compensation equation. Benefits such as health insurance, retirement contributions, stock options, bonuses, and vacation time significantly impact your total compensation.

**Timing Is Key:** Negotiate after an offer is made but before you accept. This is when you have the most leverage as the employer has already invested time and resources in selecting you.

**Articulate Your Case:** Prepare to explain why you deserve the salary and benefits you're requesting. Highlight your skills, accomplishments, and market research to substantiate your ask.

**Practice Makes Perfect:** Rehearse your pitch. Be ready to clearly and confidently express your value and articulate your compensation package expectations.

# Practical Implementation

1. **Prepare Your Pitch:**

   - Compile your list of accomplishments, skills, and results.

   - Draft a clear statement that encapsulates your value proposition.

2. **Research Thoroughly:**

   - Gather data on average salaries and benefits in your field, for your role.

   - Understand industry standards and where you fit into the spectrum.

3. **Consider the Full Range of Benefits:**

   - Make a list of benefits and perks that matter to you outside of the base salary.

4. **Simulate Negotiations:**

   - Conduct mock negotiations with a friend or mentor.

   - Anticipate possible counteroffers and objections, and prepare responses.

5. **During Negotiations:**

   - Be polite and maintain a positive tone throughout the negotiation process.

   - Use your research to back up your requests.

   - Be clear about what you want, but also show flexibility.

6. **Handling 'No':**

   - If met with resistance, ask for specific feedback or consider negotiating other benefits.

○ Have a minimum acceptable offer in mind and be prepared to walk away if necessary.

## Consistency and Evaluation

• **Regular Check-Ins:** Review your compensation package regularly against your performance and industry standards. Seek feedback from mentors and peers. Adjust your expectations and preparation accordingly for future negotiations.

• **Long-Term Perspective:** Consider how current negotiations will impact your future career trajectory. Think beyond immediate gains.

• **Document Everything:** Keep a record of agreements from negotiations. This can protect your interests and serve as a reference for future discussions.

Following these steps ensures that you approach salary and benefits negotiations informed, prepared, and with the best chance of success. Whether you're starting a new job or seeking a raise, remember that negotiations are a natural part of career advancement. Be clear, be confident, and communicate your worth effectively.

# DEBT DEMYSTIFIED: GOOD DEBT VS. BAD DEBT

## The Key Ideas

Debt doesn't inherently have to be a negative aspect of your financial journey. Understanding the differences between "good debt" and "bad debt" is crucial in harnessing debt's potential to build wealth versus letting it derail your financial stability.

- **Good Debt**
  - Invests in your future
  - Has potential for increased net worth or income
  - Is manageable within your budget
  - Examples: mortgages, student loans, business loans
- **Bad Debt**
  - Decreases in value immediately after purchase
  - Does not contribute to income or fiscal growth
  - Carries high interest rates, can lead to financial strain
  - Examples: credit card debt, high-interest personal loans, payday loans

Differentiating between the two types of debt can be nuanced:

- **Interest Rates**: Lower rates often characterize good debt.

- **Returns**: Assess the potential return on investment for taking on the debt.

- **Purpose**: Understanding the purpose behind incurring debt determines its quality.

Always consider these aspects before committing to any form of borrowing.

## Practical Implementation

1. Evaluate the necessity of the debt before you commit.

2. If investing in education or real estate, analyze potential ROI. For education, consider the career prospects in your field of study. For housing, consider the housing market trends.

3. Optimize your credit score to secure loans with the most favorable terms.

4. Develop a budget that accommodates debt repayment without sacrificing essential living expenses.

5. For unavoidable bad debt, prioritize repayment to minimize interest accrual.

Financial tools and habits for implementation:

- **Debt-to-Income Ratio**: Monitor this ratio carefully to ensure it remains at a manageable level.

- **Emergency Fund**: Build a fund to avoid bad debt in unforeseen circumstances.

- **Extra Payments**: When feasible, make additional payments to principal amounts to reduce interest over time on good debt.

# Consistency and Evaluation

Maintaining consistency in managing debt is paramount. Regular reviews should involve:

- Monitoring your total debt levels, ensuring they don't creep up.

- Reassessing interest rates, seeking refinancing opportunities when they arise.

- Evaluating your financial goals. As these evolve, so too might your definition of good and bad debt.

To ensure continual improvement:

1. **Track Your Progress**: Regularly check your debts, documenting reductions in your total debt load.

2. **Adjust as Needed**: Life changes, and so might your debt strategy. Adapt your repayment plans accordingly.

3. **Seek Advice**: Professionals can offer insights specific to your situation.

In conclusion, good debt can be a lever to success, whereas bad debt can lead to financial distress. Understand them, use them wisely, and stay in control of your financial future.

# STUDENT LOANS: STRATEGIES FOR EFFICIENT REPAYMENT

## The Key Ideas

Paying off student loans can be a daunting task, but with strategic planning and smart decisions, it can become much more manageable. The core principles to efficient repayment include understanding your loans, choosing the right repayment plan, making payments on time, considering refinancing options, and exploring forgiveness programs. Each of these components plays a crucial role in the journey towards financial freedom.

## Practical Implementation

**Understand Your Loans:**

- Importantly, know the types of loans you have, their interest rates, and the loan providers.

- Familiarize yourself with the terms and conditions of each loan.

**Choose the Right Repayment Plan:**

- Federal loans come with multiple repayment plans. Evaluate each to find one that aligns with your financial situation.

  - Standard Repayment Plan

  - Graduated Repayment Plan

  - Income-Driven Repayment Plans

**On-Time Payments:**

- Set up autopay to ensure payments are never missed.

- Autopay could also potentially lower your interest rate.

**Extra Payments:**

- Apply any extra money—bonuses, tax returns, or gifts—toward your loan principal.

- Specify extra payments go to the principal, not a future monthly installment.

**Refinancing:**

- Consider refinancing if you have high-interest loans. Refinancing can potentially lower your interest rate and monthly payment.

- Carefully compare the terms of new loan offers with your current loans.

**Loan Forgiveness:**

- Look into Public Service Loan Forgiveness (PSLF) if you work in a qualifying public service job.

- Teachers, government workers, and employees of certain nonprofits may be eligible.

**Budget Adjustment:**

- Adjust your budget to prioritize loan repayments.

- Reduce non-essential expenses to allocate more funds to your loans.

## Consistency and Evaluation

Consistency in payments is as crucial as the repayment strategy itself. Regular evaluation of your repayment progress is vital to ensure you're on track or if your strategy needs tweaking. Update your budget and repayment plan annually or whenever you experience a significant change in your financial situation.

**Regular Evaluation:**

- Monitor your loan balance and recalibrate repayment strategies as necessary.

- Always keep an eye out for new loan forgiveness opportunities or changes in federal loan policies.

**Avoiding Setbacks:**

- Never ignore communication from your loan servicer. If you're facing financial difficulties, reach out immediately to discuss options like deferment or forbearance.

**Final Thoughts:**

- Stay informed about your loans.

- Take a proactive approach to repayment.

- Remember, student loan repayment is a marathon, not a sprint. Patience and persistence pay off.

# CREDIT SCORES: BUILDING AND MAINTAINING YOUR FINANCIAL REPUTATION

## The Key Ideas

Understanding credit scores is vital for your financial health. A credit score is a numerical expression based on the analysis of your credit files, representing your creditworthiness. The higher the score, the more favorable conditions you're likely to receive on loans and credit cards. These scores are calculated using factors like payment history, credit utilization, length of credit history, new credit, and types of credit used.

**Core Principles:**

- Payment History: Making payments on time is crucial.

- Credit Utilization: High balances can negatively affect your score.

- Credit Age: Older credit accounts show long-term responsibility.

- Diverse Credit Types: A mix of account types can bolster your score.

- New Credit: Too many inquiries in a short period can be harmful.

To build and maintain a robust financial reputation, it's important to develop responsible credit habits early on and maintain them consistently.

## Practical Implementation

To ensure your credit score reflects your financial dependability, here's a practical playbook:

**Building Your Score:**

1. **Start Small**: Obtain a secured credit card or a small loan with a co-signer if necessary.

2. **Timely Payments**: Always pay your bills on time; set reminders or automate payments.

3. **Credit Mix**: Consider different types of credit, like a student loan, auto loan, or mortgage.

4. **Watch Credit Utilization**: Aim to keep balances below 30% of your credit limits.

5. **Educate Yourself**: Read your credit report annually and dispute any inaccuracies.

**Maintaining Your Score:**

- **Regular Monitoring**: Check your credit score periodically.

- **Limit New Credit**: Apply for new credit sparingly.

- **Update Information**: Ensure your personal information is current on your credit report.

- **Steady Management**: Continue to use credit responsibly over time.

# Consistency and Evaluation

Maintaining a high credit score requires ongoing care:

**Consistent Habits:**

- Track your expenses and budget accordingly.

- Regularly check account statements for accuracy.

- Keep old accounts open to lengthen your credit history.

**Periodic Evaluation:**

- Review your credit report for changes.

- Adjust based on life events, like a job change or large purchase.

- Re-evaluate your credit strategy annually to adapt to any new financial goals.

A strong credit score is your passport to financial opportunities, and it demands persistent attention and revisiting, much like a garden requires regular weeding and watering to flourish.

# RENTING VS. BUYING: THE MILLENNIAL HOUSING DILEMMA

## The Key Ideas

Renting and buying each offer unique advantages and drawbacks. Your choice depends on personal circumstances, financial status, and long-term goals.

**Renting:**

- **Flexibility:** Ideal for those who move frequently or are uncertain about job stability.

- **No Maintenance Costs:** The landlord is typically responsible for repairs and upkeep.

- **Lower up-front costs:** Renters avoid the initial down payment and closing costs.

**Buying:**

- **Building Equity:** Monthly payments contribute to ownership, not a landlord's pockets.

- **Stability:** Homeownership offers a sense of permanence and control over one's living space.

- **Potential for Appreciation:** Homes can increase in value over time, potentially yielding a profit upon sale.

Consider market conditions, rent-to-price ratios, and local economic forecasts when making a decision.

## Practical Implementation

1. **Assess Your Finances:**

   - Check your credit score.

   - Calculate your debt-to-income ratio.

   - Save for a down payment, if buying.

2. **Analyze Lifestyle Needs:**

   - Determine if your job or lifestyle requires mobility.

   - Consider the importance of living in a specific location.

3. **Research:**

   - Investigate local housing markets.

   - Compare costs of renting vs. buying similar properties.

4. **Plan for the Future:**

   - Estimate future financial changes.

   - Project potential property value growth or decline.

5. **Consult Professionals:**

   - Speak with a financial advisor.

   - Get a mortgage pre-approval, if considering buying.

6. **Make a Decision:**

   - Weigh pros and cons.

   - Choose based on logic, not emotion.

# Consistency and Evaluation

Establish a timeline for reviewing your housing situation, whether annually or in sync with major life changes. Reassess and recalibrate your decision as needed based on newer financial and personal information.

- **Keep Track:**

    ○ Monitor changes in personal finance.

    ○ Reevaluate market conditions regularly.

- **Set Milestones:**

    ○ If renting, identify savings goals towards home ownership, if desired.

    ○ If buying, target mortgage reduction or home upgrade goals.

- **Adjust as Needed:**

    ○ Remain open to switching from renting to buying, or vice versa, as your scenario evolves.

Maintain a balance between flexibility and the pursuit of long-term financial benefits. Regularly ask yourself if your current living situation aligns with your financial and lifestyle aspirations.

# HEALTH IS WEALTH: INVESTING IN INSURANCE

## The Key Ideas

Good health is the bedrock of personal prosperity. Not only does it enable you to enjoy life and tackle its challenges, but it also reduces potential financial loss from medical expenses. Buying insurance is a powerful way to safeguard your wealth, allowing you to be prepared for unforeseen health issues without draining your savings.

**Health Insurance:** Start with a comprehensive health plan. Ensure it offers adequate coverage for a range of medical services and has a reasonable deductible.

**Disability Insurance:** This is crucial. It provides you income when you're unable to work due to illness or injury.

**Long-Term Care Insurance:** As life expectancy rises, so does the need for long-term care. Invest early to get better rates.

**Critical Illness Insurance:** It offers a lump sum if diagnosed with a severe illness, such as cancer or heart attack.

**Life Insurance:** It's not just about your health but also the well-being of those who depend on you. Life insurance can cover debts, funeral costs, and provide financial security to your family.

# Practical Implementation

1. **Assess Your Needs:** Look at your lifestyle, health history, and financial situation. Ask yourself what you need to protect.

2. **Research Options:** Use online tools or consult with insurance experts. Compare different plans and providers.

3. **Read the Fine Print:** Understand what is covered and what is not. Look at the claim process, exclusions, and benefits limit.

4. **Budget for Premiums:** Incorporate insurance costs into your monthly budget. It is an investment, not an expense.

5. **Apply Young and Healthy:** Premiums are lower when you're young and in good health. Don't wait for a crisis.

# Consistency and Evaluation

**Review Annually:** Your needs will change. Regularly evaluate your insurance policies to ensure they still fit.

**Keep Up With Life Changes:** Marriage, children, and major financial changes should trigger a review of your insurance needs.

**Measure Your Insurance Investment:** Periodically check the performance of your insurance investments. Ask yourself if they're delivering the protection you expected.

**Stay Informed:** Changes in laws and insurance policies can impact your coverage. Keep abreast of these changes.

Health is indeed your wealth. By treating insurance as an investment, you'll secure not just your financial future but also peace of mind for you and your loved ones. Being proactive is key. Take charge, make informed decisions, and you'll build a safety net that supports your journey to financial independence.

# MARRIAGE AND MONEY: FINANCIAL PLANNING WITH YOUR PARTNER

## The Key Ideas

**Mutual Financial Goals:** Narrow down on your long-term objectives. Do you foresee buying a house, starting a family, or saving for early retirement? Joint goals are the engine of productive financial planning.

**Communication is King:** Regular, honest dialogues about money ward off conflicts. It's vital to build a culture of open communication about budgets, spending habits, and financial aspirations.

**Budgeting Together:** Craft a budget that reflects collective priorities. A shared budget ensures you're both steering the financial ship in harmony.

**Debt Management:** If one or both of you have debt, work out a debt-reduction strategy together. Assess each other's debts transparently and decide on the best repayment method.

**Savings Strategy:** Agree on a savings rate that aligns with your joint comfort level and goals. This might be a percentage of income or a fixed monthly sum.

**Investment Approach:** Collaborate on an investment plan that suits your joint risk tolerance and timelines. Investment decisions should be made in unison, with an eye towards diversification and long-term growth.

**Emergency Fund:** Establish an emergency fund to cover unexpected expenses. Aim for three to six months' worth of living expenses and decide on the fund's accessibility.

## Practical Implementation

1. **Set a "Money Date":** Schedule regular meetings to discuss finances without distractions.

2. **Joint Accounts or Separate?:** Decide whether to combine finances, maintain separate accounts, or a hybrid. There's no one-size-fits-all answer.

3. **Automate Where Possible:** Automate bill payments, savings, and investments to avoid forgetfulness and ensure consistency.

4. **Create an Actionable Budget:** Use tools or apps to design a budget you can track and follow.

5. **Develop a Debt Reduction Plan:**

   - List out all debts

   - Choose a payoff strategy (snowball or avalanche method)

   - Set clear payoff milestones

6. **Establish Clear Savings Goals:**

   - Identify savings goals

   - Determine monthly savings

   - Automate transfers to savings accounts

7. **Invest Together:**

    - Align on investment goals and risk tolerance

    - Select a diversified mix of investments

    - Regularly review and adjust your investment portfolio

8. **Build an Emergency Fund:**

    - Determine the total target amount

    - Decide on the account type

    - Automate contributions

# Consistency and Evaluation

**Track and Adjust:** Monitor progress with monthly check-ins. Assess if you're on track towards your goals and tweak your plans as necessary.

**Celebrate Milestones:** Acknowledge when you reach key financial milestones. This reinforces positive behavior and teamwork.

**Annual Financial Review:** Once a year, do a comprehensive review of your financial health. This includes revisiting your joint goals and adjusting for any life changes.

**Professional Guidance:** Consider consulting a financial planner for personalized advice, especially for complex situations like estate planning or investments.

Remember, financial planning as a couple is not a one-time event, but an ongoing journey. With commitment and open communication, you can navigate this path successfully together.

# FINANCIAL PLANNING FOR SINGLE MILLENNIALS

## The Key Ideas

### Prioritize Saving Early

- Compounding interest works in your favor when you start early.

- Aim to save a minimum of 20% of your earnings.

- Establish an emergency fund covering 3-6 months of expenses.

### Embrace Budgeting

- Budgeting is your roadmap to financial freedom.

- Identify needs vs. wants and allocate funds accordingly.

- Utilize budgeting apps to track expenses effortlessly.

### Invest in Your Future

- Retirement may seem distant but preparing now is crucial.

- Take advantage of employer 401(k) matches.

- Diversify through IRAs, index funds, and other investments.

### Understand Debt

- Student loans and credit cards are common but manageable.

- Prioritize high-interest debt to save on interest payments.

- Consider debt consolidation or refinancing for better rates.

### Insurance is Essential

- Health, renters, and auto insurance safeguard against financial shocks.

- Disability insurance is often overlooked but vital.

### Pursue Additional Income Streams

- Side hustles can bolster earnings and diversify income.

- Explore passive income opportunities.

## Practical Implementation

### Create a Financial Plan

1. Document your income and monthly expenses.

2. Set short-term and long-term financial goals.

3. Establish a monthly savings target.

### Effective Budgeting Techniques

- Employ the 50/30/20 rule: necessities, wants, savings.

- Regularly review and adjust your spending habits.

### Investment Strategies

- Start with low-cost index funds for simplicity and diversification.

- Consider robo-advisors for automated investing tailored to your risk tolerance.

### Handling Debt

- Use the debt snowball or avalanche methods for efficient repayment.

- Always pay more than the minimum due.

### Choose the Right Insurance

- Compare insurance policies for coverage and cost.

- Bundle policies when possible for discounts.

### Expand Income Sources

- Utilize skills or hobbies to create a profitable side business.

- Invest in learning new skills that can increase earning potential.

## Consistency and Evaluation

### Track Your Progress

- Monthly check-ins on budget and savings.

- Adjust financial strategies as your income or goals change.

## Stay Informed

- Continue learning about financial products and market changes.

- Rebalance investment portfolios annually.

## Measure Success

- Set benchmarks for savings and investment goals.

- Reflect on financial mistakes or wins to make informed decisions moving forward.

Remember, financial planning is an ongoing process that adapts with your circumstances. Keep it simple, stay disciplined, and consistently review your plan to create a secure financial future.

# TECHNOLOGY AND FINANCE: LEVERAGING APPS AND ONLINE TOOLS

## The Key Ideas

In the digital era, personal finance management has evolved from pen-and-paper ledgers to sophisticated online tools and applications. The interplay between technology and finance is more robust than ever, offering opportunities for individuals to manage their finances more efficiently and make informed decisions.

- **Tech as an Enabler**: Technology acts as a catalyst, making financial services more accessible and user-friendly.

- **Apps for Budgeting**: There are various applications designed to simplify budgeting, tracking spending, saving, and investing.

- **Online Investing Platforms**: These platforms open doors to stock markets and other investment opportunities with minimal entry barriers.

- **Automation in Saving**: Automated savings tools can help you consistently set aside money without the need for manual transfers.

- **Financial Education**: Online resources provide endless learning materials to increase financial literacy.

Technology streamlines finance, giving you control over personal economic outcomes. Embrace the tools at your disposal to achieve financial clarity and independence.

## Practical Implementation

To leverage technology for managing finances, consider the following steps:

1. **Assess Your Needs**: Define your financial goals, whether it's budgeting, saving, investing, or debt management.

2. **Research and Selection**: Research the best apps and online tools tailored to your specific needs.

3. **Setup and Integration**: Incorporate selected technology into your daily financial routines.

4. **Security Measures**: Ensure all platforms follow rigorous security protocols to protect your financial data.

5. **Regular Usage**: Engage regularly with the apps and tools to stay on top of your finances.

6. **Keep Abreast of Updates**: Financial technologies evolve rapidly; keep an eye out for updates and new features that can further assist your financial management.

Leveraging these tools means not just having them on your phone or computer, but actively using them to make real-time, data-driven decisions about your financial future.

## Consistency and Evaluation

Maximizing the benefits of financial tech tools requires consistent use and regular evaluation of their impact.

• **Daily Habits**: Incorporate app check-ins into your daily routine. Regular monitoring can flag issues early.

• **Performance Analysis**: Monthly reviews of your financial progress can underscore areas for improvement.

• **App Reassessments**: Annually assess whether your chosen tools still fit your evolving financial landscape.

• **Result Sharing**: Share your financial successes and setbacks with a community or mentor for accountability and advice.

For a maximized technology-finance synergy, maintain diligence and flexibility, adapting your strategies to find what works best for your unique financial situation.

# SIDE HUSTLES AND THE GIG ECONOMY: DIVERSIFYING YOUR INCOME

## The Key Ideas

In today's fast-paced world, relying solely on a full-time job is no longer the safest bet for financial security. Diversifying your income streams is crucial, and one practical way to do this is by engaging in side hustles and participating in the gig economy.

- **Diverse Income Streams:** Having multiple income streams can help cushion the blow if you lose your primary source of income and gives you financial flexibility.

- **Flexibility and Autonomy:** With side hustles, you often get to choose when and how much you work, allowing for better work-life balance.

- **Skill Development:** Pursue gigs that allow you to build on your talents and passions, which can lead to career growth and personal fulfillment.

- **Financial Goals:** Employing a side hustle can pave the way to meet financial goals quicker, be it paying off debt, saving to buy a house, or planning for retirement.

# Practical Implementation

To successfully integrate side hustles into your income strategy, start with these steps:

1. **Assess Your Skills:** Identify what you're good at and how you can monetize those skills.

2. **Research Opportunities:** Look for gigs that resonate with your expertise and interests. Popular platforms include: Upwork, Etsy, and Airbnb.

3. **Start Small:** Test the waters with small projects to understand what works best for you.

4. **Legal and Tax Implications:** Stay informed about any legal or tax obligations associated with your side hustle.

**Best Practices**

• **Set Clear Goals:** Know why you're starting a side hustle and what you hope to achieve.

• **Time Management:** Balance your full-time job, side hustle, and personal life by managing time efficiently.

• **Networking:** Leverage social media and professional networks to promote your services.

• **Quality Over Quantity:** Prioritize tasks that add the most value and income.

# Consistency and Evaluation

The final step in creating a sustainable side hustle is ensuring consistency and regularly evaluating your progress.

• **Regular Monitoring:** Keep track of your earnings and adjust your strategies as needed.

• **Reinvest in Your Hustle:** Use a portion of your earnings to grow your side business.

• **Seek Feedback:** Use client or customer feedback to improve your offerings.

• **Know When to Fold:** If a side gig isn't working out, don't be afraid to cut losses and try something new.

Remember, success in the gig economy doesn't happen overnight. Keep your expectations realistic, stay persistent, and continuously refine your approach to diversifying your income.

# CONSCIOUS CONSUMERISM: ALIGNING YOUR VALUES WITH YOUR SPENDING

## The Key Ideas

Conscious consumerism is a practice where you make purchasing decisions based on the impact they have on the environment, health, society, and economy. It involves being fully aware of how your consumption habits align with your personal values. To practice this, follow these principles:

- **Understand Your Impact**: Recognize that each purchase has a ripple effect, influencing demand, production methods, and resource allocation.

- **Value-based Spending**: Prioritize products and services that resonate with your ethical, environmental, and social values.

- **Quality Over Quantity**: Opt for items that are made to last, reducing the need for frequent replacements.

- **Transparency**: Research brands to ensure they practice what they preach regarding labor rights, environmental policies, and corporate responsibility.

- **Local and Small Businesses**: Support local economies by buying from smaller producers whenever possible.

• **Mindful Consumption**: Question the necessity of each purchase to avoid unnecessary accumulation of goods.

## Practical Implementation

Implementing conscious consumerism into your daily life might seem daunting, but you can do it through incremental changes:

1. **Budget for Values**: Allocate a portion of your budget specifically for products and services that align with your values.

2. **Research Before Buying**: Invest time to understand a product's lifecycle, from raw materials to production, to distribution.

3. **Use Apps and Resources**: There are numerous apps and resources to help you easily evaluate a company's practices.

4. **Initiate Conversations**: Talk to vendors about sourcing and ethical practices; your interest can influence their choices.

5. **Prioritize Experiences**: Invest in experiences rather than things. They often bring greater joy and less wastefulness.

6. **Eco-Friendly Alternatives**: Whenever possible, replace single-use items with sustainable alternatives.

## Consistency and Evaluation

Conscious consumerism requires regular reflection and evaluation:

• **Monthly Assessments**: Review your spending monthly to see if it aligns with your values and goals. Adjust as needed.

• **Stay Informed**: Industries and brands evolve. Keep up with the latest news about their practices.

• **Community Engagement**: Join forums or groups of like-minded individuals to support and get support in your conscious consumption journey.

• **Be Patient with Yourself**: Change takes time. Celebrate small victories and learn from lapses without self-reprimand.

# PRIORITIZING EXPERIENCES OVER POSSESSIONS

## The Key Ideas

**Experiential Richness Over Material Wealth** Society often associates success with the accumulation of possessions. Yet lasting satisfaction arises not from what we own, but from what we experience. Material items can become obsolete, but experiences enrich your life narrative and evolve into memories that define you.

**Investing in Experiences is Investing in Yourself** Allocating funds towards experiences such as travel, education, or hobbies sparks personal growth. It cultivates skills, broadens horizons, and enhances social relationships. Unlike possessions, experiences become part of your identity.

**The Diminishing Returns of Materialism** While basic needs are non-negotiable, the quest for the latest gadget or fashion item provides only a temporary uplift in happiness. Over time, the excitement fades, leading to a perpetual cycle of consumption and dissatisfaction.

# Practical Implementation

1. **Budget for Experiences**

   - Allocate a portion of your income to an 'Experience Fund'.

   - Plan for big-ticket experiences like travel or significant events well in advance.

2. **Embrace Minimalism**

   - Evaluate possessions based on their utility and joy they bring.

   - Sell or donate items that are no longer meaningful, reducing clutter and potentially adding to your 'Experience Fund'.

3. **Gift Experiences**

   - Instead of material gifts, offer experiences such as concert tickets, classes, or vouchers for shared activities.

   - Encourages stronger connections with others and supports a less materialistic culture.

4. **Cultivate Free Experiences**

   - Seek out free events, parks, and community experiences.

   - Understand that enriching experiences don't always have a price tag.

5. **Document Your Experiences**

   - Keep a journal or create albums of your experiences.

   - These records reinforce the value of your experiences and can be revisited to rekindle joy.

6. **Mindful Consumption**

   ○ Purchase items with longevity and timeless value.

   ○ Be intentional with material possessions, seeing them as tools to enhance experiences.

## Consistency and Evaluation

**Track Your Experiential Investments** Regularly monitor your spending. Ensure that you are investing more in experiences than in fleeting material goods. Reflect on how these experiences have contributed to your personal growth and happiness.

**Evaluate Your Satisfaction** Periodically, assess your level of contentment and compare periods of materialistic versus experiential spending. Recognize patterns that lead to sustained joy.

**Evolve Your Approach** As your life changes, so too might your definition of meaningful experiences. Continuously adapt your priorities to align with your evolving self.

**Share and Inspire** Cultivating an experiential mindset can influence your social circle positively. Share your journey and inspire others to prioritize experiences over possessions.

# INVESTMENTS 101: UNDERSTANDING STOCKS, BONDS, AND MUTUAL FUNDS

## The Key Ideas

Investing is a critical component of wealth-building, especially for millennials who are shaping their financial futures. Diving into the investment world can be overwhelming, but understanding the basics of stocks, bonds, and mutual funds sets a strong foundation.

**Stocks** represent ownership in a company. When you buy stock, you become a shareholder and have a claim on part of the company's assets and earnings. The value of stocks can rise and fall based on company performance, market trends, and other economic factors.

- **Advantages of stocks:** potential for high returns; dividends; ownership in a company.

- **Risks of stocks:** market volatility; no guaranteed returns; potential for loss.

**Bonds** are essentially loans you give to a company or government. In return, they agree to pay you back the principal amount on a specified date and make regular interest payments.

- **Advantages of bonds:** steady income through interest payments; generally lower risk than stocks.

- **Risks of bonds:** interest rate changes can affect value; potential for default.

**Mutual Funds** are investment vehicles that pool money from many investors to purchase a diversified portfolio of stocks, bonds, or other securities. This diversification reduces risk, making mutual funds a popular choice for many investors.

- **Advantages of mutual funds:** professional management; diversification; affordability.

- **Risks of mutual funds:** management fees; less control over individual investments; performance no guarantee.

## Practical Implementation

To navigate these investments, begin with clear financial goals. Are you saving for retirement, a home, or creating passive income streams? Your timeline and risk tolerance will guide your strategy.

1. **Research**: Understand individual stocks, bonds, and mutual fund offerings. Tools like financial news, reports, and analytical platforms provide insights.

2. **Diversify**: A balanced portfolio of stocks, bonds, and mutual funds can manage risk. Avoid putting all your eggs in one basket.

3. **Start small**: Ease into investing with amounts you're comfortable with, potentially using robo-advisors or apps tailored for beginners.

4. **Monitor progress**: Regularly check your investments to ensure they align with your goals. Rebalance as necessary.

Implementing a systematic investment plan can smooth out market volatility through dollar-cost averaging, where you invest a fixed amount regularly regardless of the market condition.

# Consistency and Evaluation

A disciplined approach is key. Regularly contribute to your investments and review your portfolio:

- **Annual Review**: Check your portfolio's performance against your goals. Adjust as needed.

- **Economic Changes**: Stay informed about economic trends that could affect your investments.

- **Balance and Rebalance**: Your asset allocation should change as you approach your financial targets.

Remember, investing is a marathon, not a sprint. Patience, consistent investment, and regular evaluation will help you make informed decisions and work toward your financial goals.

By adhering to these principles, millennials can build a robust investment portfolio that provides security and growth potential. Keep in mind, the journey is unique to your personal financial situation—it's your wealth and your future.

# THE POWER OF COMPOUND INTEREST: STARTING EARLY MATTERS

## The Key Ideas

Compound interest shapes the backbone of sound personal finance strategy—it's the silent engine propelling your investments to exponential growth over time. Imagine a snowball rolling down a hill, growing larger as it picks up more snow. Compound interest works similarly, where the initial investment is your snowball, and the extra snow is the interest that continues to accumulate onto itself. Starting early maximizes this effect, reaping benefits that are significantly larger than those realized by those who start investing later in life.

- **Time is Your Ally**: The earlier you start saving and investing, the more you allow compound interest to work its magic.

- **Reinvestment and Growth**: The interest earned isn't merely to be spent; but reinvested, thereby earning more interest.

- **Exponential Growth**: Given enough time, and thanks to the rate at which compound interest grows, small initial investments can lead to vast sums.

# Practical Implementation

Initiating your journey with compound interest is more about forming good habits and less about the initial amount. Here's how you can start:

1. **Open a Savings or Investment Account**: Choose a high-interest savings account or a solid investment vehicle like an index fund with low fees.

2. **Set Up Automatic Contributions**: Even a modest monthly amount can burgeon into substantial savings over time. The key is consistency.

3. **Increase Contributions Over Time**: As your income grows, proportionally increase your investment contributions.

4. **Avoid Unnecessary Withdrawals**: Let your investments stay invested to maintain the compound interest trajectory.

5. **Diversify Wisely**: A mix of stocks, bonds, and other assets can protect you during market fluctuations and keep your compounding engine stable.

Each step is a building block towards a future where your financial wellbeing is significantly buffered by the decisions you make today.

# Consistency and Evaluation

Establishing a regular review of your financial strategy is crucial to making the power of compound interest work effectively. Every quarter, consider these steps:

- **Review Your Contributions**: Can you afford to save more? Then do it. Every little bit counts.

- **Examine Your Portfolio's Performance**: Ensure it aligns with your risk tolerance and financial goals.

- **Adapt as Necessary**: Life changes and so should your financial strategy. Always stay informed and be ready to adjust.

In conclusion, early investment leveraging compound interest sets the foundation for solid financial health. Start as soon as you can, stay consistent, and regularly reassess your strategy. The power of compound interest is in the patience and prudence it rewards. Remember, when it comes to compound interest, time is the most valuable asset you have. Use it wisely.

# RETIREMENT ACCOUNTS: ROTH IRA VS. TRADITIONAL IRA

## The Key Ideas

Understanding the fundamental differences between Roth IRAs and Traditional IRAs is pivotal to effective retirement planning. Here's what you need to know:

- **Tax Treatment**: Contributions to Traditional IRAs may be tax-deductible, reducing taxable income for the year they are made. The withdrawals, however, are taxed at ordinary income rates. In contrast, Roth IRA contributions are made with after-tax dollars and thus do not offer an immediate tax benefit, but qualified distributions during retirement are tax-free.

- **Withdrawal Rules**: Roth IRAs offer more flexibility with no required minimum distributions (RMDs) during the owner's lifetime, whereas Traditional IRAs mandate RMDs starting at age 72.

- **Eligibility**: Roth IRA contributions are subject to income limits, while Traditional IRAs do not limit contributions based on income but do have age restrictions for deductibility if you or your spouse are covered by a retirement plan at work.

- **Early Withdrawal Penalties**: Both accounts typically impose a 10% penalty on distributions taken before age 59 ½, with certain exceptions. Roth IRAs allow for contribution withdrawals at any time without penalties or taxes, a feature not available with Traditional IRAs.

## Practical Implementation

Taking action on your retirement plan involves several practical steps:

1. **Evaluate Your Tax Bracket**: Consider whether you anticipate being in a higher tax bracket now or during retirement. If you expect higher taxes later, Roth may be a better option.

2. **Analyze Your Income**: Stay aware of the Roth IRA income limits which might influence your eligibility for contribution.

3. **Decide When To Pay Taxes**: If you prefer paying taxes now to avoid uncertainty in the future, lean towards a Roth. If you want to defer taxes and possibly reduce your current taxable income, consider a Traditional IRA.

4. **Set Up An Account**: Choose a brokerage or financial institution to open your IRA. Ensure it supports the investments you're interested in.

5. **Invest According to Your Risk Tolerance**: Use the IRA to invest in a diversified mix of assets aligned with your risk tolerance and retirement timeline.

## Consistency and Evaluation

Maintaining and periodically assessing your retirement strategy is crucial. Remember to:

- **Review annually**: Check your contributions and adjust as needed to maximize your retirement savings. Consider converting from a Traditional to a Roth IRA if your situation changes.

• **Balance portfolios**: Diversify between different types of IRAs to hedge against tax rate fluctuations.

• **Monitor regulations and limits**: Stay up-to-date with IRS rules and contribution limits, as they could impact your retirement strategy.

• **Evaluate your financial situation regularly**: As your income or family situation changes, your retirement planning should adapt accordingly.

• **Seek Professional Advice**: Consult with a financial advisor to help tailor your retirement strategies to your unique situation.

In summary, choosing between a Roth IRA and a Traditional IRA requires an understanding of tax implications, access to funds, and future financial outlook. Make informed choices and revisit them regularly to ensure a secure retirement.

# NAVIGATING EMPLOYER-SPONSORED RETIREMENT PLANS LIKE 401(K)S

## The Key Ideas

Before diving deep into the mechanics of 401(k)s, it's essential to grasp the fundamental principles.

### Tax Advantages

Understand the primary benefit of 401(k) plans: **tax deferral**. Contributions are made pre-tax, reducing taxable income and allowing investments to grow tax-free until retirement.

### Employer Match

Many employers offer a match on your contributions. This is essentially *free money* and maximizing this benefit should be a priority.

### Investment Options

Familiarize yourself with the range of investment choices offered within your 401(k). These could vary from conservative bonds to more aggressive stock funds.

**Vesting Schedules**

Be aware of your plan's vesting schedule, which determines when you gain full ownership of employer-contributed funds.

**Fees and Expenses**

Pay attention to the fees associated with the management of your 401(k) account and individual investment options.

## Practical Implementation

Taking actionable steps is critical. Here's how to effectively engage with your 401(k):

- **Start Contributing Early**: Time in the market is more important than timing the market. Begin with what you can afford and increase contributions over time.

- **Maximize Employer Match**: Contribute at least enough to get the full match. It's an immediate 100% return on your contribution.

- **Allocate Wisely**: Align your investment choices with your risk tolerance and retirement timeline. Consider target-date funds for hands-off investing.

- **Keep Costs Down**: Opt for low-fee index funds when possible. High fees can eat into your retirement savings over time.

- **Increase Contributions**: Whenever you receive a pay raise, boost your 401(k) contributions accordingly.

- **Avoid Early Withdrawals**: Withdrawing funds before retirement can result in taxes and penalties.

## Consistency and Evaluation

Long-term success with your 401(k) hinges on regular assessment and consistency:

- **Review Annually**: At least once a year, assess your portfolio's performance and adjust if necessary.

- **Stay the Course**: Market fluctuations are normal. Avoid the temptation to react emotionally to market volatility.

- **Plan for the Future**: As you approach retirement, gradually shift to more conservative investments to preserve capital.

Remember, the 401(k) is a powerful tool for building retirement wealth, but it requires informed, proactive management. By adhering to these guidelines, you can optimize your retirement savings and secure a more comfortable future.

# REAL ESTATE INVESTING: IS IT RIGHT FOR YOU?

## The Key Ideas

Real estate investing can seem like a golden path to wealth generation, but it's essential to discern if it aligns with your financial goals, risk tolerance, and commitment level.

- **Understanding the Real Estate Market**: Markets can fluctuate dramatically, and understanding cycles is fundamental.

- **Types of Real Estate Investments**: From rental properties to REITs, know the various investment vehicles.

- **Capital Requirement**: Real estate often requires a significant upfront investment.

- **Passive vs. Active Investment**: Decide how much time you can dedicate to managing the investment.

- **Risk Assessment**: Factor in market risks, property damages, and vacancy rates.

- **Long-term Perspective**: Real estate investment is typically a long-term commitment.

- **Tax Considerations**: Be informed about the tax benefits and liabilities.

# Practical Implementation

To translate these key ideas into action, you must take calculated steps:

1. **Education**: Immerse yourself in learning about real estate through books, courses, and seminars.

2. **Financial Review**: Analyze your finances to determine how much you can safely invest.

3. **Market Analysis**: Research local markets for property value trends, rental demand, and economic stability.

4. **Network Building**: Connect with real estate agents, experienced investors, and financial advisors.

5. **Investment Strategy Development**: Outline clear goals and an investment plan that prioritizes your financial security.

6. **Property Selection**: Identify properties that align with your strategy and budget.

7. **Due Diligence**: Thoroughly investigate the property's condition, legalities, and potential expenses.

8. **Financing**: Explore your options for mortgages, loans, or real estate partnerships for funding.

9. **Management Plan**: Decide whether to self-manage or hire a property management company.

# Consistency and Evaluation

Investing in real estate requires a steady hand. Regular evaluation of your investment's performance is vital.

- **Set Benchmarks**: Establish clear metrics for success and review them annually.

• **Portfolio Reassessment**: Consistently reassess your investment to ensure it meets your financial goals.

• **Staying Informed**: Keep abreast of market changes and adjust your strategy accordingly.

• **Professional Consultations**: Regularly consult with a financial advisor or property manager to refine your approach.

In conclusion, real estate investing may be a profitable venture if approached with diligence, patience, and a comprehensive understanding of the market. Ensure each decision aligns with your financial goals and doesn't compromise your financial security.

# CUTTING-EDGE INVESTING: CRYPTOCURRENCIES AND STARTUPS

## The Key Ideas

Investing in cryptocurrencies and startups represents a thrilling opportunity to be part of the innovation that's defining the future of finance and technology. This chapter focuses on the essentials of navigating these dynamic markets.

- **Cryptocurrencies:** Digital currencies that employ encryption to secure transactions and control the creation of new units.

    - Decentralization is key, with no single entity controlling the network.

    - The value is determined by supply, demand, and market sentiment.

    - Blockchain technology underpins most cryptocurrencies, ensuring transparency and security.

- **Startups:** Companies in their early stages, often innovation-driven and poised for rapid growth.

    - The potential for high returns accompanies a high risk of failure.

○ Investments often help startups grow and achieve milestones towards profitability.

Both fields are characterized by volatility and the potential for high returns, making them attractive for those willing to accept the risks.

## Practical Implementation

**Starting with Cryptocurrencies:**

1. **Education is Critical:** Understand the technology, read whitepapers, and follow industry news.

2. **Set a Budget:** Invest only what you can afford to lose.

3. **Diversify:** Don't put all your eggs in one basket.

4. **Choose Reliable Exchanges:** Research and use exchanges with strong security measures.

5. **Storage:** Decide whether a hot wallet (connected to the internet) or a cold wallet (offline storage) suits your needs better.

6. **Long-Term vs Short-Term:** Have clear objectives for your investment timeframe.

**Investing in Startups:**

1. **Research is Key:** Get to know the industry, the business model, and the team behind the startup.

2. **Start Small:** Consider starting with smaller angel investments or joining a syndicate.

3. **Growth Potential:** Look for startups with scalable business models.

4. **Legal Considerations:** Check the legal implications and your rights as an investor.

5. **Exit Strategy:** Understand the long-term plan for the startup and your investment.

## Consistency and Evaluation

To succeed in cutting-edge investments, regularly review your portfolio and stay informed about market trends.

- **For Cryptocurrencies:**

  - Track the performance and news related to your holdings.

  - Be prepared to adjust your positions as the market changes.

- **For Startups:**

  - Monitor company progress through updates and milestones.

  - Watch for signs of growth or distress, reassessing your investment as needed.

**Evaluation** involves a consistent process of checking in on your investments' status against your financial goals, the current economic climate, and adjusting as necessary.

- **Risk Management:** Regularly assess if the level of risk you're taking aligns with your long-term financial goals.

- **Performance Review:** Measure the performance of your investments against benchmarks and industry standards.

- **Stay Updated:** Keep abreast of new developments in legislation, technology, and market shifts that might impact your investments.

In conclusion, while investing in cryptocurrencies and startups can offer substantial rewards, it demands a disciplined approach focused on continuing education, risk management, and regular evaluation. Approach these opportunities with a blend of enthusiasm and informed prudence to navigate these modern financial landscapes.

# RISK MANAGEMENT: HOW TO BALANCE A DIVERSE PORTFOLIO

## The Key Ideas

**Diversification:** The core of risk management in any portfolio is diversification. This concept means spreading your investments across various asset classes, industries, and geographies to reduce the impact of any single failing investment.

**Asset Allocation:** Allocate assets based on your risk tolerance, investment horizon, and financial goals. Each asset class has its own risk and return characteristics, and an ideal portfolio incorporates an appropriate mix for your specific situation.

**Correlation:** Understand the relationship between the assets in your portfolio. Investing in assets that have a low or negative correlation with each other can help mitigate risk since they are unlikely to move in the same direction at the same time.

**Regular Rebalancing:** Over time, the value of individual investments will change, potentially altering the intended asset allocation. Regular rebalancing keeps your portfolio aligned with your desired risk level.

**Risk Assessment:** Regularly assess your risk tolerance. As personal circumstances or market conditions change, so too may your comfort with risk.

# Practical Implementation

1.  Start by assessing your financial goals. Determine the return necessary to achieve these goals within your time horizon.

2.  Evaluate your risk tolerance. Are you a risk-seeker or risk-averse? This self-assessment will guide how you allocate your investments.

3.  Establish your asset allocation. Divide your portfolio among asset classes like stocks, bonds, and cash, or sub-categories like small-cap stocks, high-yield bonds, and international assets.

4.  Select investments within each asset class. For example, within equities, consider various sectors like technology, healthcare, and energy.

5.  Utilize low-cost index funds or ETFs. They offer easy access to diversification and come with the added benefit of passive management and lower fees.

6.  Schedule regular portfolio reviews. At least annually, reassess your portfolio to ensure it remains in line with your goals and risk tolerance.

7.  Rebalance as needed. If your allocations deviate significantly from your plan, bring your portfolio back into balance by purchasing underweighted assets or selling overweighted assets.

# Consistency and Evaluation

**Set Clear Benchmarks:** Track your portfolio performance against relevant benchmarks. This could be a major stock index, a blend of indices representing your portfolio's composition, or a predefined return goal.

**Consistent Review:** Engage in a routine review process, looking beyond the simple returns and understanding the volatility and correlations within your portfolio.

**Adaptation:** Be prepared to adjust your strategy as markets evolve. Financial landscapes change, and your portfolio should be dynamic enough to adapt without straying from your long-term objectives.

**Risk Monitoring:** Keep abreast of changes in market conditions, legislation, and global events that could impact your investments. Quick responses to these changes can be the difference between preserving wealth and suffering significant losses.

Remember, a well-balanced portfolio is not a set-it-and-forget-it proposition; it is a dynamic collection of investments that you must actively manage and adjust to suit your changing needs and the changing world.

# PASSIVE INCOME: BUILDING WEALTH WHILE YOU SLEEP

## The Key Ideas

Passive income is a term that means earning money without active involvement. It's not a shortcut to wealth but a strategic approach that requires thoughtful selection, an initial investment of either time or money, and sometimes a measure of patience. Think of passive income as a garden—you plant the seeds, nurture them, and eventually reap the harvest without having to sow every single day.

**Diverse Streams**: Don't rely on a single source of income. The more diverse your passive income streams, the better your chances of building significant wealth.

**Investment versus Involvement**: While some passive income sources require upfront financial investment (e.g., dividend stocks, rental property), others demand time or expertise (e.g., writing a book or creating an online course).

**Tax Implications**: Understand the tax consequences of your passive income—some streams are more tax-efficient than others.

**Risks and Rewards**: Evaluate the risk associated with each passive income stream. A high return often comes with high risk.

**Automation**: Leverage technology and automation to minimize your active involvement in passive income streams.

## Practical Implementation

1. **Identify Your Skill Set**: Leverage what you're good at. If you're a talented writer, consider an e-book. Skilled in a particular craft? Sell your creations online.

2. **Research Your Options**:

   - Real Estate Investment Trusts (REITs)

   - Dividend-paying stocks

   - Peer-to-peer lending platforms

   - Online business or blog

3. **Analyze Your Capital**: Determine how much money or time you can afford to invest.

4. **Start Up Small**: Start with a low-cost investment option to understand the process and limit risk.

5. **Automate Investments**: Use apps and online tools to automate stock purchases or contributions to investment accounts.

6. **Use High-Interest Savings Accounts**: Place your emergency funds or savings in high-yield accounts to earn more with minimal effort.

7. **Educate Yourself Continuously**: Stay informed on investment strategies and market trends.

# Consistency and Evaluation

*Consistency* in maintaining and reviewing your passive income streams is crucial. Set regular intervals, like quarterly reviews, to assess performance and make adjustments.

*Specifically*:

-**Track Changes**: Note any alterations in the market or the performance of your income stream that may necessitate adjustments to your strategy. -**Readjust Priorities**: If a particular stream is underperforming consistently, reconsider its place in your portfolio. -**Growth-Focused**: Always look for ways to expand your passive income streams without increasing your active involvement significantly.

*Evaluation Criteria*:

- Income Growth: Is the passive income stream growing over time?

- Time Investment: Are you still within your preferred level of involvement?

- Performance Against Goals: Is the income stream meeting your financial objectives?

In pursuing passive income, approach with diligence and patience. While it won't make you rich overnight, it can significantly propel you towards financial security and independence. Embrace the practical steps, consistently apply them, and you can build wealth while you indeed rest easy.

# TAXES: PLANNING AND SAVING STRATEGIES

## The Key Ideas

Taxes, often perceived as unavoidable and complex, offer opportunities for savings through strategic planning.

1. **Understanding Taxes**: Comprehend how your income is taxed; recognize the differences between marginal and effective tax rates.

2. **Retirement Accounts**: Maximize contributions to tax-advantaged retirement accounts like Roth IRA and 401(k).

3. **Tax Deductions and Credits**: Identify deductions and credits applicable to your situation, such as educational expenses or charitable donations.

4. **Investment Tax Planning**: Utilize tax-efficient investment vehicles and strategies to minimize capital gains taxes.

5. **Health Savings Accounts (HSAs)**: For those with high-deductible health plans, HSAs offer triple tax advantages.

6. **Timing Income and Deductions**: Control the timing of income and deductions to optimize tax liability across years.

# Practical Implementation

To harness these concepts, begin with a thorough review of your financial situation. Use these steps for practical implementation:

1. **Gather Records**: Compile all financial statements, including income, investments, and expenses.

2. **Forecast Tax Liability**: Project your tax for the year using online calculators or software.

3. **Contribute to Retirement Accounts**: Prioritize maximum contributions to IRAs and 401(k)s before the deadline (usually April 15th of the next year).

4. **Leverage Deductions and Credits**:

   ○ Itemize deductions if they exceed the standard deduction.

   ○ Claim all eligible credits, such as the American Opportunity Tax Credit for education costs.

5. **Assess Investments**:

   ○ Hold investments for at least a year to benefit from lower long-term capital gains tax rates.

   ○ Consider tax-loss harvesting to offset gains with losses.

6. **Utilize HSAs**: Contribute to an HSA if you're eligible, using it for medical expenses or as an additional retirement account.

7. **Income and Deduction Timing**:

   ○ If expecting a higher income next year, accelerate deductions into the current year.

   ○ Conversely, defer income when possible to avoid moving into a higher tax bracket.

# Consistency and Evaluation

A consistent approach and regular assessment are critical. Here's how to maintain and evaluate your tax planning strategy:

- **Quarterly Review**: Check your tax situation quarterly to make adjustments for life changes, income fluctuations, or tax law updates.

- **Annual Assessment**: At each year's end, measure your strategy's effectiveness. Did you reduce your taxable income? Have you utilized all possible deductions and credits?

- **Professional Advice**: For complex situations, consult a tax professional to ensure compliance and optimize savings.

- **Stay Informed**: Tax laws change. Stay abreast of updates that could affect your planning.

In conclusion, proactive tax planning is integral to personal finance management. By understanding and applying these strategies, you can significantly reduce your tax burden and bolster your wealth over time. Remember, tax planning is a year-round activity, not just an end-of-year rush.

# ESTATE PLANNING: IT'S NOT JUST FOR THE WEALTHY

## The Key Ideas

Estate planning often conjures images of vast wealth and sprawling estates. However, it's a crucial process for everyone, not just the affluent. Here's why:

- **Asset Distribution**: Estate planning helps dictate how your assets are distributed, safeguarding your wishes irrespective of your asset level.

- **Family Protection**: It offers clarity and guidance to your loved ones, eliminating uncertainties during difficult times.

- **Legal Costs and Taxes**: A well-structured estate plan can minimize legal fees and taxes, maximizing what your beneficiaries receive.

- **Healthcare Directives**: It includes making decisions about your medical care should you become incapacitated.

- **Guardianship**: If you have minor children, estate planning is essential for appointing their guardians.

Understanding these facets illuminates that estate planning is about care and protection, not just wealth.

# Practical Implementation

Engaging with estate planning does not have to be overwhelming. Here's how you can get started:

1.  **Inventory Your Assets**: List every asset you own, however modest it may be. This includes bank accounts, investments, insurance policies, real estate, and personal property.

2.  **Define Your Wishes**: Specify who receives what. If you don't, the state will make these decisions for you, which may not align with your desires.

3.  **Choose Your Proxies**: Pick trustworthy individuals to make decisions on your behalf for healthcare and finances should you be unable to do so yourself.

4.  **Draft Essential Documents**: Create a will, a durable power of attorney, and healthcare directives with clear instructions.

5.  **Keep Beneficiary Designations Updated**: Ensure your retirement accounts and life insurance policies reflect your current beneficiaries.

6.  **Consult a Professional**: Seek advice from an estate planner or attorney to ensure compliance with laws and maximize tax advantages.

7.  **Communicate Your Plan**: Talk openly with your family about your estate plan to prevent surprises and conflict.

Remember, this isn't a one-off task. Life changes, and so should your estate plan.

# Consistency and Evaluation

Estate planning is not a static endeavor. It's vital to review and adjust your plan regularly:

- **Annual Checkups**: Make it a habit to review your estate plan yearly or with significant life changes like marriage, divorce, the birth of a child, or acquiring new assets.

- **Stay Informed**: Tax laws and regulations can change. Stay abreast of these modifications and evaluate how they may affect your estate plan.

- **Monitor Relationships**: Your chosen executors or proxies today may not be the right choice tomorrow. Reassess these roles as relationships evolve.

- **Assess Asset Values**: As your wealth grows or shifts, ensure your plan reflects your current financial picture.

- **Record Keeping**: Keep all estate planning documents in a secure but accessible location and inform your executors where to find them.

An up-to-date estate plan ensures that your intentions are clear and actionable, providing peace of mind for both you and your loved ones.

# SOCIALLY RESPONSIBLE INVESTING: MAKING AN IMPACT WITH YOUR MONEY

## The Key Ideas

Socially responsible investing (SRI) merges investment decisions with ethical values. Essentially, it allows you to grow your wealth while also contributing positively to the world. Here are the key points you need to understand:

- **Definition and Scope**: SRI means choosing investments based on not only financial returns but also social and environmental impact. It encapsulates various strategies, including impact investing, environment, social, and governance (ESG) integration, and shareholder advocacy.

- **Screening Methods**: Investments are screened based on positive criteria (inclusionary) such as renewable energy initiatives, or negative criteria (exclusionary) like avoiding industries such as tobacco or firearms.

- **Financial Returns**: Historical data suggests SRI can match or even outperform traditional investments. Reduced risk from better corporate practices often underpins this performance.

- **Evolving Landscape**: SRI is not a static field; it evolves as societal values change. Staying informed is crucial.

# Practical Implementation

For implementation, consider a step-by-step approach:

1. **Clarify Your Values**: Reflect on what matters most to you. Environment? Social justice? Animal welfare? This helps tailor your investment choices.

2. **Research**: Look for funds or companies that align with your values. Tools and resources like MSCI ESG ratings or Morningstar's Sustainability Rating can guide you through this process.

3. **Financial Planning**: Align your SRI choices with your financial goals. Remember, diversification remains essential.

4. **Professional Advice**: Consider consulting a financial advisor familiar with SRI for tailored investment strategies.

5. **Start Small**: Dip your toes with a small portion of your portfolio. You can adjust as you become more comfortable and informed.

6. **Monitoring Performance**: Keep an eye on both the financial performance and the ethical impact of your investments. Online platforms and apps now offer detailed reports on both fronts.

## Consistency and Evaluation

It's important to regularly review your SRI portfolio, ideally on an annual basis, to ensure alignment with your values and financial objectives. Check for changes in:

- Performance against benchmarks.

- Business practices of the entities you've invested in.

- Your personal values or financial goals.

When evaluating, here's what to focus on:

- **Performance Data**: Review returns and compare them with traditional benchmarks to assess financial health.

- **Impact Reporting**: Use available reports to evaluate the real-world impact of your investments.

- **Advocacy and Voting**: If you own shares directly, exercise your right to vote on shareholder resolutions and engage in advocacy.

Remember, financially savvy decisions made with a clear conscience can drive both individual prosperity and collective progress. Socially responsible investing is no longer a niche; it's a powerful movement reshaping the financial landscape.

# LEARNING FROM FINANCIAL FAILURES: BOUNCING BACK WITH RESILIENCE

## The Key Ideas

Financial setbacks are not the end of the road but rather a bend that leads to more knowledgeable and strategic planning. The grit to overcome hurdles and the capacity to learn from financial failures are what forge the resilience required for long-term financial health.

**Acknowledge and Analyze:** Start with accepting that the setback happened. It is a normal part of engaging with financial markets and decisions. Closely analyze what led to the failure. Was it a lack of research, overconfidence, or external factors beyond your control? Understanding the root cause is essential.

**Realign Goals:** Upon recognizing the factors that caused the financial setback, it's imperative to reassess and adjust your financial goals. If necessary, set more realistic or short-term targets to rebuild confidence and traction.

**Educate Yourself:** Use the setback as motivation to bolster your financial literacy. Seek knowledge about risk management, diversification, and the psychological elements of investing. Knowledge is a powerful tool for prevention.

**Risk Mitigation Strategies:** Implement strategies to manage and mitigate risks in the future. This can include setting stop-loss orders, diversifying investments, and maintaining an emergency fund.

## Practical Implementation

To bounce back effectively from financial failures, take the following practical steps:

1.  **Create a Recovery Plan:** Draft a plan that outlines clear, achievable steps to regain financial stability. Define timeframes and set milestones.

2.  **Budget Re-evaluation:** Revisit your budget to identify areas for cost savings. This might mean cutting unnecessary expenses or finding more affordable alternatives.

3.  **Debt Management:** If debt contributed to the financial setback, develop a strategy to manage and reduce it. Prioritize debts with higher interest rates.

4.  **Savings Strategy:** Rebuild your savings through regular, consistent contributions, even if they are small. Over time, they add up and provide financial security.

5.  **Seek Professional Advice:** Don't hesitate to consult with financial advisors or counselors. Their expertise can be invaluable in navigating complex financial landscapes.

6.  **Practice Emotional Discipline:** Train yourself to detach emotions from financial decisions. Emotional reactions can lead to rash decisions that may exacerbate financial losses.

# Consistency and Evaluation

Building financial resilience requires consistent effort and regular evaluation:

- **Track Progress**: Keep a diligent record of your financial activities and regularly check them against your recovery plan to ensure you are on track.

- **Maintain Financial Discipline**: Stay committed to your budget, savings, and investment strategies. Discipline is key for financial recovery and future success.

- **Regularly Reassess Risks**: Continuously evaluate the risk levels of your financial endeavors. Adjust your strategies as needed to minimize potential losses.

- **Adapt to Change**: Be prepared to adjust your financial plan as personal circumstances or market conditions change.

By consistently applying these practices, you are not only working towards recovering from failure but are also laying a robust foundation for a financially secure future. Remember, resilience isn't about never failing; it's about learning and evolving with each challenge that comes your way.

# FINANCIAL ADVISORS: WHEN AND HOW TO SEEK PROFESSIONAL HELP

## The Key Ideas

- **Identify Your Financial Needs:** Understand your financial goals, whether it's debt management, investment strategies, retirement planning, or another area where professional guidance can be beneficial.

- **Know When to Seek Help:** Common triggers include a major life event like marriage, children, or a career change, feeling overwhelmed by financial decisions, or a significant increase in income or assets.

- **Choosing the Right Advisor:** Look for credentials such as CFP (Certified Financial Planner) or a reasonable fee structure, such as fee-only services to avoid conflicts of interest.

- **Check Their Background:** Verify the advisor's history with regulatory bodies like the SEC or FINRA to ensure they have a clean record.

- **Prepare for the First Meeting:** Have a clear understanding of your financial situation and be ready to communicate your goals and concerns.

# Practical Implementation

1. **Assess Your Financial Health:** Take stock of your income, debts, assets, and investments. Accurate self-assessment aids in pinpointing the type of advice needed.

2. **Self-Educate Beforehand:** A baseline understanding of financial concepts helps you communicate effectively with an advisor and understand their recommendations.

3. **Interview Multiple Advisors:** Don't settle for the first one you meet. Ask questions about their experience with clients similar to you and how they've overcome financial challenges.

4. **Understand Their Offerings:** Financial advisors offer varying services. Ensure the advisor's offerings align with your needs.

5. **Agree on Communication:** Decide on how frequently you wish to communicate with your advisor. This could be quarterly, semi-annually, or annually.

6. **Cost Transparency:** Request a clear outline of how they are paid. Whether it's hourly, a flat fee, or a percentage of assets under management, it should be straightforward.

7. **Documented Plan:** Insist on a written plan or strategy that covers your discussed goals and their proposed solutions.

# Consistency and Evaluation

- **Set Regular Check-ins:** Determine a schedule for reviewing your financial progress with your advisor. Consistency helps in adjusting to any life or market changes.

- **Measure Progress Against Goals:** Regularly evaluate whether your financial goals are being met and if the advice given is leading to measurable improvements.

- **Adapt As Needed:** Be willing to make adjustments to your financial plan or change advisors if your needs are not being met or if your circumstances change.

- **Seek Second Opinions:** If you're unsure about the advice provided, don't hesitate to consult another professional for comparison.

In summary, seeking the help of a financial advisor becomes critical when you're facing financial complexity or major life changes. Choose your advisor carefully, ensure your goals are clearly defined and understood, and maintain a consistent review schedule to stay on track. Remember, the right advisor should act as a partner in achieving your financial aspirations while keeping your best interests front and center.

# STAYING INFORMED: THE IMPORTANCE OF FINANCIAL EDUCATION

## The Key Ideas

Financial education equips you with the knowledge necessary to make informed money management decisions, ensuring financial stability and success. Here are the fundamental concepts that underscore the importance of financial literacy:

- **Financial Goals**: Understanding different financial objectives, such as saving for retirement, creating an emergency fund, or buying a home, shapes how you manage money.

- **Budgeting**: Learning to budget effectively allows you to control spending, save more, and avoid unnecessary debt.

- **Investing Principles**: Knowledge of investment strategies and vehicles can result in increased wealth over time and help secure a financial future.

- **Credit Management**: Understanding credit, credit scores, and debt management minimizes costly borrowing and improves financial health.

- **Taxation**: Awareness of tax implications can lead to significant savings and proper compliance with tax laws.

- **Risk Management**: Insurance and other risk management strategies are essential to protect against financial hardship due to unforeseen events.

- **Retirement Planning**: Early and informed planning for retirement secures future financial independence.

- **Market Trends**: Keeping abreast of economic conditions and market trends helps in making timely and prudent financial decisions.

## Practical Implementation

To move from understanding to action, follow these steps:

1. **Set Clear Goals**: Define what you want to achieve financially in both the short and long term.

2. **Create a Budget**: Track your income and expenses. Prioritize savings and necessary spending over wants.

3. **Educate Yourself**: Read books, take online courses, attend workshops, or consult a financial advisor to enhance your understanding of financial matters.

4. **Start Investing**: Begin with small, manageable investments. Use tax-advantaged retirement accounts like Roth IRAs or 401(k)s.

5. **Review Credit Reports**: Annually check your credit reports for accuracy to manage and improve your credit score.

6. **Plan for Taxes**: Take advantage of tax credits and deductions. Consult a tax advisor if necessary.

7. **Get Insured**: Obtain appropriate insurance policies (health, life, property) to safeguard against potential losses.

8. **Stay Updated**: Regularly read financial news and updates to stay informed about the economic environment.

# Consistency and Evaluation

Maintaining a disciplined approach to financial education requires regular self-assessment and adjustment:

- **Monitor Progress**: Regularly review financial goals and budget to ensure you are on track with your objectives.

- **Adjust Budgets**: As financial circumstances change, recalibrate your budget to reflect new income levels or expenses.

- **Evaluate Investments**: Assess investment portfolios annually, reallocate assets based on performance and changing financial goals.

- **Update Knowledge**: Financial markets and laws evolve. Keep learning to ensure your financial plans remain relevant.

- **Seek Professional Advice**: If financial situations become complex, don't hesitate to seek professional guidance.

By integrating the importance of financial education into your daily life, you'll be equipped to manage your finances with insight and confidence. Stay disciplined, stay informed, and remember that every step you take is a stepping stone towards a secure financial future.

# MONEY AND MENTAL HEALTH: NAVIGATING STRESS AND ANXIETY

## The Key Ideas

Financial concerns frequently trigger stress and anxiety. Understanding the psychological impact of monetary issues is the first step toward mental well-being. Here, we'll explore how financial strain affects your mental health and introduce methods to mitigate this stress.

• Financial stress is an emotional experience connected to the anxiety or fear of not having enough money.

• Money-related anxiety can lead to a range of mental health challenges, including depression and anxiety disorders.

• The stress from dealing with debt or struggling to make ends meet can affect sleep, concentration, and relationships.

• Recognizing warning signs, such as unusual spending habits or constant worry about money, is crucial.

# Practical Implementation

Implement these strategies to manage financial stress effectively:

1. **Create a Budget**

   - Itemize income and expenses.

   - Prioritize needs over wants.

   - Allocate funds to savings, even if small.

2. **Emergency Savings Fund**

   - Aim to save three to six months of expenses.

   - Automate savings to make it consistent.

3. **Debt Management**

   - Pay off high-interest debt first.

   - Consider consolidation or negotiation for lower rates.

4. **Mindfulness and Self-care**

   - Practice relaxation techniques like deep breathing or meditation.

   - Ensure adequate sleep, nutrition, and exercise.

5. **Seek Professional Advice**

   - Financial advisor for tailored advice.

   - Therapist or counselor for coping strategies.

6. **Educate Yourself**

   - Read books or articles on personal finance.

   - Attend workshops or seminars.

# Consistency and Evaluation

Maintaining a healthy relationship with money is an ongoing process:

- **Regular Review of Financial Plan**: Monthly check-ins.

- **Adjust Budget as Needed**: Life changes; so should your budget.

- **Set Realistic Goals**: Short-term victories lead to long-term success.

- **Track Mental Health Symptoms**: Journaling or mental health apps.

- **Community Support**: Support groups or online forums.

Craft a realistic plan, be patient with your progress, and don't hesitate to seek help when necessary. Your financial and mental health will benefit from your proactive approach.

# FINANCIAL INDEPENDENCE, RETIRE EARLY (FIRE): THE MILLENNIAL DREAM?

## The Key Ideas

Financial Independence, Retire Early (FIRE) is more than just a trendy buzzword; it's a lifestyle movement with growing appeal among millennials. The core concept is simple: save and invest aggressively so you can retire much earlier than traditional retirement plans suggest. Typically, it requires saving around 50-70% of your income, which can seem daunting, but the promise of early retirement drives many to embrace frugality and maximize their earnings.

- **Aggressive Savings**: Aim for a high savings rate, around 50-70% of your income.

- **Investing Wisely**: Invest your savings smartly to enable compound growth.

- **Frugal Living**: Reduce expenses wherever possible without sacrificing quality of life.

- **Income Maximization**: Look for ways to increase your earning potential.

• **Retirement Calculation**: Plan how much you need to retire early, considering factors like withdrawal rates and future expenses.

# Practical Implementation

1. **Budgeting Basics**

2. Identify and categorize all of your expenses.

3. Cut non-essential spending.

4. Use budgeting tools like spreadsheets or apps for tracking.

5. **Saving Strategies**

6. Automate savings to ensure consistent contributions.

7. Establish an emergency fund.

8. Take advantage of tax-efficient accounts like Roth IRAs or 401(k)s.

9. **Investment Principles**

10. Diversify investment across stocks, bonds, and other assets.

11. Consider low-cost index funds for long-term growth.

12. Reinvest dividends.

13. **Expense Management**

14. Emphasize value, not just cost-cutting.

15. Optimize recurring expenses such as utilities, subscriptions, and insurance.

16. **Revenue Enhancement**

17. Seek promotions or negotiate salary increases.

18. Develop side hustles or passive income streams.

# Consistency and Evaluation

To achieve FIRE, consistency is as critical as the initial planning. Regularly assess your progress and make adjustments where necessary.

- **Quarterly Reviews**: Check your savings rate, investment growth, and living expenses.

- **Annual Assessments**: Evaluate any significant changes that could impact your FIRE timeline, such as a job change, moving to a low cost of living area, or family planning.

- **Adaptability**: Be willing to adjust your plan as your life and the economy change.

Balancing present needs and future goals is vital to avoid burnout. Remember, the FIRE journey is not only about retiring early; it's about gaining financial freedom to live on your terms.

# PARENTHOOD AND FINANCES: PLANNING FOR YOUR GROWING FAMILY

## The Key Ideas

**Understanding the Cost of Parenthood** Becoming a parent is life-altering, and so are the associated finances. From prenatal care to college funds, every phase of your child's life comes with expenses. Begin by researching and understanding these costs to create a solid foundation for financial planning.

**Budgeting for a New Family Member** Adjust your budget to accommodate the new expenses. This involves revisiting and possibly revising your current financial plan to include additional costs such as childcare, healthcare, education, and daily living expenses related to raising a child.

**Emergency Fund** Anticipate the unexpected. Growing a healthy emergency fund is crucial for weathering the unforeseen expenses that come with parenthood, such as urgent medical care or sudden loss of income.

**Insurance Needs** Reevaluate your insurance coverage. With dependents, you must consider increasing your life and disability insurance to ensure your family's financial stability should anything happen to you.

**Investment in Education** Education costs are soaring. Establishing a college fund or education savings plan early on gives you a head start in securing your child's academic future without the burden of crippling debt.

**Estate Planning** It's never too early to think about the future. Create a will and appoint a guardian to protect your child's interests. Consider setting up trusts or savings accounts that can secure their financial wellbeing if you're not around.

**Government Benefits and Tax Breaks** Take advantage of tax credits, deductions, and government programs designed to aid families. These can offer significant savings and support in managing the costs of raising a child.

## Practical Implementation

1. **Budget Adjustment**

   - Analyze current expenses and income.

   - Identify new expenses related to the child.

   - Revise your budget to include these costs, prioritizing essentials.

2. **Emergency Fund Strategy**

   - Aim to save at least three to six months' worth of living expenses.

   - Set up automatic transfers to a dedicated savings account.

3. **Insurance Review**

   - Consult with an insurance advisor to adjust policies to your new needs.

   - Ensure that coverage amounts will support your child through adulthood.

4. **Education Fund Planning**

   ◦ Research education savings options like 529 plans or Coverdell ESA.

   ◦ Regularly contribute to the selected plan to take advantage of compounding interest.

5. **Estate Plan Development**

   ◦ Work with an attorney to draft a will.

   ◦ Consider setting up a trust for your child's inheritance.

6. **Maximizing Governmental Benefits**

   ◦ Educate yourself on available child-focused tax credits and deductions.

   ◦ Apply for government programs that support child healthcare and nutrition if eligible.

## Consistency and Evaluation

**Review Financial Plans Annually** Circumstances change, and so should your financial plan. An annual review ensures that you remain aligned with long-term goals and are prepared for the costs of each developmental stage of your child's life.

**Child-Related Expense Tracking** Maintain a dedicated record of all child-related expenses. This helps in understanding the actual costs of raising a child and can inform future budgeting decisions.

**Performance Assessment of Education Fund** Monitor the growth of your education fund. Regular checks allow you to make necessary adjustments to meet the rising costs of education.

**Reassess Insurance and Estate Plans** As your child grows, their needs may change. Regularly reassess your insurance coverage and estate plan to ensure they continue to meet your family's needs.

In conclusion, approaching parenthood with a clear financial strategy paves the way for a secure future for your family. Remember: plan smartly, act consistently, and reassess frequently to address the evolving financial needs of your growing family.

# TRAVEL AND MONEY: EXPLORING THE WORLD WITHOUT BREAKING THE BANK

## The Key Ideas

### Budgeting for Travel

- Determine the cost of your dream destinations and create a savings plan.

- Incorporate travel into your monthly budget, designating funds specifically for this purpose.

### Smart Travel Choices

- Opt for countries with lower living costs yet rich cultural experiences.

- Travel during the off-peak season to benefit from lower prices and fewer crowds.

### Travel Hacking

- Learn the art of travel hacking to earn and redeem points and miles for free or discounted travel.

- Use credit cards that offer travel rewards and sign up bonuses wisely.

### Economical Accommodations

- Stay in hostels, guesthouses, or rent private rooms through services like Airbnb.

- Consider longer-term stays for discounts and a deeper dive into local living.

### Local Living

- Eat like a local, shopping at markets and eating at local restaurants rather than tourist spots.

- Use public transportation, bicycle rentals, or walk when possible.

## Practical Implementation

1. **Setting Travel Goals**

   - Identify specific travel goals and the typical cost associated with each destination.

   - Prioritize experiences over luxury; focus on what truly enriches you culturally and personally.

2. **Creating a Travel Budget**

   - Analyze your income and expenses to allocate savings for travel.

   - Implement tools such as budgeting apps to track your progress.

3. **Understanding Travel Hacking**

   - Research credit cards offering the best travel rewards; apply for one or two that suit your habits and credit score.

   - Stay informed about promotions, partnerships, and point redemption opportunities.

4. **Leveraging Accommodation Options**

   - Use comparison websites to find deals on accommodations.

   - Look for opportunities to house sit, or swap homes with someone in your destination country.

5. **Immersing Yourself in Local Culture**

   - Research local customs, festivals, and free events.

   - Use apps to find recommendations from locals.

6. **Sustainable Travel Practices**

   - Consider taking longer trips less frequently to reduce your carbon footprint and delve deeper into the culture.

   - Engage in volunteering or work exchange programs—these can offset some travel costs while contributing to local communities.

# Consistency and Evaluation

- **Track Your Spending** Keep meticulous records of travel spending to ensure you stay within your budget.

- **Reward Points Evaluation** Quarterly assess the value you're getting from your points and adjust your strategy if necessary.

- **Post-Trip Review** After each trip, review what worked well with your budgeting and what didn't. Learn from this to refine for next time.

- **Adjusting Goals and Expectations** Life and financial situations change. Regularly revisit your travel goals to ensure they align with your current finances and priorities.

- **Continuous Learning** Stay updated on evolving travel hacks and changes in the travel industry to maximize your resources.

In aligning with your goals of exploring the world without breaking the bank, remember it's all about finding a balance between the experiences you crave and the financial health you need. Achieving this means planning, adaptability, and an unquenchable thirst for adventure and cultural immersion—affordably.

# AUTOMATING YOUR FINANCES FOR EFFICIENCY AND PEACE OF MIND

## The Key Ideas

Automating your finances means setting up systems that handle financial activities on your behalf, reducing the need for manual intervention and minimizing the chance of human error. Here's why it's crucial:

1. **Consistency**: Regular, automated contributions to savings and investment accounts help build wealth over time.

2. **Timeliness**: Automated bill payments ensure bills are paid on time, avoiding late fees and maintaining a good credit score.

3. **Budget control**: By automating the allocation of your income, you stick to your budget and avoid overspending.

4. **Emotional relief**: Removing the emotional aspect of transferring money into savings leads to better financial decisions.

## Practical Implementation

Implementing financial automation involves several steps that are both easy to set up and highly beneficial in the long run.

**Setting Up Automatic Transfers**

*Schedule recurring transfers* from your checking to your savings or investment accounts. Timing these after payday ensures that saving isn't an afterthought.

**Automating Bill Payments**

• Set up *Direct Debits* for fixed expenses (e.g., mortgage, utilities).

• Use your bank's bill-paying service or the biller's automatic payment feature for variable expenses.

**Key tip:** Always ensure you have a buffer in your checking account to avoid overdraft fees.

**Automating Debt Repayments**

Prioritize high-interest debt and set up automatic payments that are more than the minimum due to accelerate debt reduction.

**Continuous Investing**

• Utilize *employer-sponsored retirement plans* with automatic paycheck deductions.

• Consider *robo-advisors* for automatic rebalancing and investment in low-cost index funds.

**App-Based Automation**

Use financial apps that round up purchases to the nearest dollar and automatically invest the spare change.

### Reducing Manual Oversight

- Leverage alerts for low balances or large transactions to stay informed without constant monitoring.

- Create a separate email account for financial matters to streamline communication and reduce noise.

## Consistency and Evaluation

### Staying Consistent

- **Revisit your automation settings** regularly to ensure they align with your financial goals.

- **Adjust for life changes** such as a pay raise, a new job, or a change in family size.

### Evaluating Effectiveness

- Perform a *quarterly review* of your financial statements to assess progress.

- Calculate your net worth periodically to monitor overall financial health.

**Remember:** Financial automation is a tool, not a set-it-and-forget-it solution. Stay engaged, but let technology handle the day-to-day tasks. This will free up your time and mind for the more important aspects of life, while you steadily work towards financial independence.

# THE ILLUSION OF KEEPING UP: AVOIDING LIFESTYLE INFLATION

## The Key Ideas

Lifestyle inflation refers to the phenomenon where your spending on non-essential items increases along with your income. It often goes unnoticed as earnings grow over time, leading to a cycle where increased income doesn't necessarily equate to increased wealth. The crux here is to distinguish between wants and needs, focusing on long-term financial health rather than immediate gratification.

• **Understand your spending triggers**: Recognize what prompts you to spend unnecessarily and identify ways to avoid these triggers.

• **Set clear financial goals**: Decide what you want your future to look like and let that vision guide your spending habits.

• **Budget wisely**: Allocate funds to different areas of your life, prioritizing savings and investments.

• **Avoid debt**: Minimize the use of credit unless it's for well-considered, appreciating investments.

• **Stay grounded**: Frequently remind yourself of your long-term objectives versus short-term desires.

# Practical Implementation

To effectively avoid lifestyle inflation, implement the following strategies:

1. **Track your expenses**: Use apps or spreadsheets to monitor where your money is going each month. This keeps you accountable.

2. **Automate savings**: Before you have the chance to spend extra income, automatically divert it into savings or investment accounts.

3. **Cultivate frugality**: Learn to appreciate value over luxury. Quality doesn't always mean expensive.

4. **Invest in yourself**: Use additional funds to improve skills or health, enhancing your ability to generate future income.

5. **Focus on experiences**: Instead of accumulating things, invest in experiences that bring lasting happiness and personal growth.

# Consistency and Evaluation

Maintaining a consistent approach toward managing your finances is crucial. Schedule regular check-ins, perhaps monthly or quarterly, to assess your financial trajectory. Adjust your budget as needed but maintain the discipline to keep savings and investments as key pillars of your financial plan.

- **Monitor cash flow**: Ensure more money comes in than goes out. Act immediately if the reverse starts to happen.

- **Review goals**: Life changes, and so might your goals. Keep them relevant and motivating.

- **Reward yourself**: When you hit a financial milestone, celebrate in a way that doesn't set you back financially.

By following these principles and strategies, you'll navigate away from the illusion of keeping up, building a resilient financial future that can withstand societal pressures to spend beyond your means.

# SUSTAINABLE LIVING: ECO-FRIENDLY CHOICES THAT SAVE MONEY

## The Key Ideas

• **Less is More**: Embrace minimalism by purchasing fewer, higher-quality items that last longer and save money over time.

• **Energy Efficiency**: Invest in energy-efficient appliances and lighting to reduce utility bills.

• **Water Conservation**: Cut water usage with low-flow fixtures and by fixing leaks promptly.

• **Transportation**: Opt for walking, biking, carpooling, or public transportation instead of solo car commutes.

• **Local and Seasonal**: Buy local, in-season produce to lower transportation emissions and cost.

• **DIY Products**: Create homemade cleaners and personal care items to avoid the premium on "green" branded products.

# Practical Implementation

1. **Audit Your Home**

   ○ Conduct an energy audit to identify areas for improvement.

   ○ Switch to LED lighting and unplug electronics when not in use.

2. **Embrace Minimalism**

   ○ Declutter and donate items.

   ○ Before buying, ask, "Do I need this? Will it last?"

3. **Conserve Water**

   ○ Install low-flow toilets and showerheads.

   ○ Collect rainwater for plants.

4. **Smarter Shopping**

   ○ Buy bulk to reduce packaging.

   ○ Choose products with less environmental impact.

5. **Sustainable Transit**

   ○ Organize a carpool roster for your workplace.

   ○ Consider an electric or hybrid vehicle.

6. **Grow Your Own**

   ○ Start a vegetable garden to save on grocery bills.

   ○ Compost kitchen scraps for free fertilizer.

# Consistency and Evaluation

• **Track Your Progress**: Use apps or spreadsheets to monitor your utility usage and expenses.

• **Make It a Habit**: Incorporate new practices one at a time until they stick.

• **Community Engagement**: Join local groups to stay informed on sustainability efforts.

• **Reflect and Adapt**: Review your actions every few months, staying open to new methods to improve efficiency.

# PROTECTING YOURSELF AGAINST FRAUD AND IDENTITY THEFT

## The Key Ideas

You are your best defense against fraud and identity theft. In today's digital age, personal information is as valuable as currency, and safeguarding it is crucial. Understanding the methods fraudsters use and recognizing the signs of identity theft are the first steps to protection.

- **Information Security**: Your personal data, such as Social Security numbers, bank account details, and passwords, should be treated with the same care as your money.

- **Digital Hygiene**: Regularly update your computer and device security software. Use robust, unique passwords and two-factor authentication wherever possible.

- **Constant Vigilance**: Monitor your financial statements and credit reports for unauthorized transactions or changes. Early detection is key.

- **Smart Sharing**: Be discerning about whom and where you share your information. Social media profiles often give away more than you realize.

- **Scam Recognition**: Know the red flags that signal scams, such as requests for immediate action, promises of unrealistic returns, or threats.

## Practical Implementation

1. **Secure Your Documents**: Keep sensitive documents in a secure place, both physically and digitally. Shred unneeded papers with personal data.

2. **Strengthen Passwords**: Use passwords that are a mix of letters, numbers, and symbols. Consider password managers for additional security.

3. **Beware of Phishing**: Never click on links or download attachments from unknown sources. Verify emails and texts that request personal information.

4. **Exercise Caution Online**: Shop on secure, reputable websites. Look for the padlock icon in the address bar indicating a secure connection.

5. **Educate Yourself**: Stay informed about current fraud and scam trends. Knowledge is power in the fight against fraudsters.

6. **Limit Exposure**: Share your Social Security number only when absolutely necessary. Be selective about the apps and services where you input personal information.

## Consistency and Evaluation

Consistently follow these practices and make them a habitual part of your financial life. Regularly evaluate the effectiveness of your strategies, adapting as necessary when new threats emerge.

- **Monthly Checks**: Review bank statements and credit card transactions each month without fail.

- **Annual Credit Reports**: Request a free credit report annually from each of the three major credit bureaus.

- **Stay Updated**: Technology and fraud tactics continually evolve. Keep your knowledge current and adjust your protections accordingly.

In conclusion, protecting yourself against fraud and identity theft is an ongoing process. Implement these measures with care, and maintain vigilance to ensure your financial well-being remains intact. Remember, the effort you put into safeguarding your information not only preserves your wealth but also your peace of mind.

# THE GIG ECONOMY AND RETIREMENT STRATEGIES: A NEW APPROACH

## The Key Ideas

**The Rise of the Gig Economy**: The gig economy has massively grown, presenting a non-traditional career path that can lead to financial flexibility but also uncertainty.

**Income Diversification**: Gig workers must diversify their income streams to buffer against the ebb and flow of gig availability.

**Retirement Planning**: Traditional retirement plans, like 401(k)s and pensions, are often not available to gig workers, necessitating a new, proactive approach.

**Investment Options**: Exploring IRAs, Solo 401(k)s, and investment in index funds and real estate can compensate for the lack of employer-sponsored retirement benefits.

**Tax Considerations**: Understanding and utilizing tax deductions and credits available to self-employed individuals can maximize earnings and retirement contributions.

# Practical Implementation

1. **Start with a Budget**:

   - Determine monthly expenses.

   - Allocate a percentage for retirement savings.

   - Utilize budgeting apps to track spending.

2. **Retirement Accounts**:

   - Open an Individual Retirement Account (IRA).

   - Consider a Solo 401(k) for higher contribution limits.

   - Invest consistently, regardless of income fluctuations.

3. **Diversification**:

   - Alternate between active gigs and passive income sources.

   - Invest in different assets (e.g., stocks, bonds, real estate).

4. **Emergency Fund**:

   - Save at least 3-6 months of expenses.

   - Prioritize liquidity and accessibility.

5. **Insurance**:

   - Obtain health insurance to avoid unforeseen medical expenses.

   - Consider disability insurance, especially critical for gig workers.

6. **Long-Term Investment**:

   - Embrace low-cost index funds for long-term growth.

   - Reinvest dividends to compound wealth.

7. **Tax Strategy**:

   ◦ Keep detailed records of income and expenses.

   ◦ Deduct home office, travel, supplies, and equipment.

   ◦ Work with a tax professional familiar with gig economy challenges.

8. **Education and Growth**:

   ◦ Continually learn new skills relevant to your gig pursuits.

   ◦ Network with fellow gig workers for opportunities and advice.

## Consistency and Evaluation

**Monitor and Adjust Your Budget**: Keep a close eye on your financial plan, adjusting as your gig work fluctuates.

**Regular Contributions**: Aim to contribute to your retirement accounts monthly. If income is variable, adjust the amount, but maintain the habit.

**Evaluate Investments**: Annually review your portfolio to ensure alignment with your retirement goals and risk tolerance.

**Adapt to Tax Law Changes**: Stay informed about changes in tax laws that may affect gig workers and adjust your strategy accordingly.

**Assess Insurance Needs**: As your situation changes, periodically reevaluate your insurance to ensure adequate coverage.

**Continuous Learning**: The gig economy evolves rapidly. Stay updated on trends and skills that increase your marketability and earning potential.

**Health Check**: At least once a year, perform a comprehensive review of your financial health, including savings rate, investment performance, and retirement projections.

# GIVING BACK: PHILANTHROPY ON A MILLENNIAL BUDGET

## The Key Ideas

Philanthropy isn't the exclusive realm of the wealthy; it is a concept that thrives on participation from all economic levels. Millennials, even on a budget, have the potential to contribute meaningfully to causes they care about. The key to philanthropy in this demographic is creativity, participation, and the understanding that small contributions can have a big impact.

- **Transcend Monetary Donations**: Recognize that giving back doesn't always mean financial aid. Volunteering time and skills often proves invaluable.

- **Micro-donations Matter**: Embrace the impact of small, regular donations. Many small contributions can accumulate to a significant amount.

- **Leverage Social Media**: Use online platforms to raise awareness or crowdfund for causes, thus amplifying philanthropic reach.

- **Planned Giving**: Budget for philanthropy, treating it as a non-negotiable expense similar to rent or groceries.

• **Legacy and Impact**: Understand that giving back is about building a legacy and driving change, regardless of donation size.

## Practical Implementation

To integrate philanthropy into a millennial budget, follow these simple steps:

1.  **Identify Passion Causes**: Pinpoint issues that resonate deeply with you. Alignment with personal values increases commitment.

2.  **Research**: Vet organizations to ensure your contributions are used effectively. Opt for those with transparent operations and measurable impacts.

3.  **Budget Allocation**: Dedicate a realistic portion of your budget to philanthropy. Even a small percentage of your income can make a difference.

4.  **Consider Recurring Donations**: Steady support often helps charities plan and operate more efficiently.

5.  **Non-monetary Contributions**: List your skills and expertise. Offer these to organizations that could benefit from them.

Here are non-monetary ways to give back:

• **Mentoring and Coaching**: Share knowledge and guidance with those coming up in your field.

• **Community Service**: Participate in local cleanups, food banks, or shelter support.

• **Goods Donation**: Give clothes, electronics, and books you no longer use to those in need.

• **Advocacy**: Raise awareness about issues and mobilize others to support the cause.

## Consistency and Evaluation

Maintaining a consistent philanthropic approach ensures a sustainable impact. Regularly review the effectiveness of your contributions and adjust as necessary.

• **Set Goals**: Establish clear, achievable goals for your philanthropic activities.

• **Track Contributions**: Keep a record of your donations and voluntary hours.

• **Reflect and Reassess**: Periodically review the outcomes your contributions have achieved.

• **Stay Informed**: Keep abreast of the issues and the organizations you support to understand their evolving needs.

• **Spread the Word**: Encourage friends and family to contribute, magnifying the collective impact.

In summary, millennial philanthropy on a budget is rooted in consistent, thoughtful contributions of time, skill, and finance to causes that align with personal values. By being resourceful, strategic, and sincere in giving back, millennials can forge significant change and create a lasting personal and social legacy.

# A CALL TO ACTION: BUILDING AND SUSTAINING WEALTH OVER A LIFETIME

## The Key Ideas

Building and sustaining wealth is not about quick wins or the latest fads. It is grounded in time-tested principles that require discipline, smart decision-making, and an understanding of finance. Below are the cornerstone ideas to achieve this goal.

- **Live Below Your Means**: Consistently spending less than you earn is fundamental. It allows you to save and invest the surplus.

- **Invest Wisely**: Learning to invest intelligently is critical. Diversify across different asset classes and avoid high-risk ventures unless they form part of a balanced portfolio.

- **Financial Literacy**: Enhance your understanding of financial concepts. Stay informed about tax strategies, investment vehicles, and retirement planning.

- **Long-Term Perspective**: Wealth building is a marathon, not a sprint. Set long-term goals and resist the temptation to deviate from them for short-term gains.

- **Avoid Debt**: High-interest debt can be a wealth-killer. Minimize debt, especially on depreciating assets, and pay off existing debt quickly.

• **Retirement Planning**: Start early, take advantage of tax-advantaged accounts, and consistently contribute to your retirement savings.

• **Estate Planning**: Ensure your wealth is protected and distributed according to your wishes through proper estate planning.

## Practical Implementation

Adopting the key ideas into your life requires a strategic approach. Here's how to get started:

1. **Create a Budget**: Categorize your expenses, differentiate needs from wants, and plan your spending. Stick to your budget to control your financial flow.

2. **Emergency Fund**: Establish a fund with at least 3-6 months of living expenses. This will help avoid debt during unexpected events.

3. **Set Financial Goals**: Define clear, measurable, and achievable financial goals. Include short-term, medium-term, and long-term objectives.

4. **Investment Education**: Invest time in learning about the stock market, mutual funds, real estate, and other investment opportunities.

5. **Automate Finances**: Automate your savings and regular investments to ensure consistency.

6. **Regular Check-ups**: Schedule monthly financial check-ups to review budgets, track spending, and assess investment performance.

7. **Seek Professional Advice**: Consider the guidance of a financial advisor for personalized investment strategies and tax planning.

# Consistency and Evaluation

Sustaining wealth over a lifetime necessitates regular evaluation and a consistent approach.

- **Monitor Progress**: Regularly track your net worth to gauge progress towards your financial goals. Adjust your strategies as needed.

- **Performance Reviews**: Assess investment performance annually. Rebalance your portfolio to align with your financial objectives and risk tolerance.

- **Lifestyle Inflation**: Be mindful of increased spending with higher income. Save and invest the additional funds instead of elevating your standard of living.

- **Continual Learning**: Keep up-to-date with financial trends, tax laws, and new investment opportunities.

- **Success Measures**: Continuously redefine what success looks like at different stages of your life and align your financial plan accordingly.

By applying these principles with persistence and discipline, you can progressively build and maintain wealth throughout your lifetime.

www.ingramcontent.com/pod-product-compliance
Lightning Source LLC
Chambersburg PA
CBHW060102260726